My Boy, Ben

A STORY OF LOVE, LOSS AND *Grace*

By David Wheaton

TRISTAN Publishing
Minneapolis

Library of Congress Cataloging-in-Publication Data
Wheaton, David, 1969-
  My Boy, Ben / written by David Wheaton.
    pages cm
  ISBN 978-1-939881-04-5 (alk. paper)
1. Labrador retriever. 2. Human-animal relationships. 3.
Pets--Death--Psychological aspects. I. Title.
  SF429.L3W49 2014
  636.752'7--dc23
                        2014009948

TRISTAN Publishing, Inc.
2355 Louisiana Avenue North
Golden Valley, MN 55427

Some names have been changed for purposes of anonymity.
Front cover photograph taken by Bruce Wheaton, David's dad.

To learn about all of our books with a message please visit
www.TRISTANpublishing.com

TABLE OF CONTENTS

Dad and Mom,

It was a special time . . .

and he was a most special dog.

David

INTRODUCTION

"That's my boy."

I whispered this often to Ben. It is curious how such a little phrase, and the gentle stroke of his head that accompanied it, could express all of my affection and admiration for him. But it did.

Ben *was* my boy . . . and he knew it. From that first August morning I held him, a soft and adorable, buff-colored Labrador puppy, to the final afternoon nearly nine years later, a deep and endearing relationship was forged between a man and his dog that brought the simplest and best of earthly joys, the depths of grief and sorrow, and ultimately, comfort and grace beyond all expectation.

He was a constant presence in my life. Whether next to my bed at night or my desk by day, whether asleep on my lap on the couch or begging food beside me at the table, whether on walks or hikes or road trips — actually, any trip in the car — Ben was just *always there*.

I used to think my inseparable bond with Ben was somewhat unique, maybe even a bit abnormal. *Are other people this connected with their dogs?* I often wondered. Sometimes I even wrestled with the extent of my love for him. *With so many people in need of love and companionship, am I investing too much of myself in a dog?*

It's easy to see why we were so close. I was a single guy in my thirties who lived alone and worked out of my home. Most days it was just Ben and me. And although I had grown up in a family that always had a dog, Ben was the first for whom I had full caretaking responsibilities — from feeding to training to exercising to looking after his health.

But the depth of my relationship with him was a result of more than solitude, time, and care. It was rooted in the kind of dog Ben was. Beyond his physical traits — his athletic build, beautiful coat, pleasing face, and almond-shaped brown eyes — it was his noble character and endearing personality that caused people to almost invariably remark, "What a sweet boy." Then the questions would begin, "Where did you get him?" "Has he always been that calm?" "Did you train him to do that?"

I tried to deflect some of the praise because I knew very well that I was merely an amateur owner who had been blessed with a truly exceptional dog—a dog of a lifetime.

* * *

Ben forever changed how I view the human-dog relationship. Dog owners span a wide spectrum on this. On one end, there are those who see their dogs in a more *utilitarian* way—to serve a specific purpose, such as protecting the livestock, retrieving the fowl, entertaining the kids, accessorizing the home . . . and then it's back to the kennel after that. A distinct and intentional separation of man and dog is maintained at all times because "it's a dog" . . . and that's that.

This is certainly not to question whether Utilitarians love their dogs, because they do. It's just that they keep them at more of an arm's-length distance than the dog owners at the other end of the spectrum—the Egalitarians, who view and treat their dogs as coequal members of the family.

Dog hair on clothes, the couch, the bed, or the front seat of the car is a minor inconvenience for Egalitarians—"It's just part of having a dog." Going anywhere without their dog would be, well, "Why go?" Licks on the face or plate aren't unhygienic ("Dogs have cleaner saliva than humans, you know.") but rather shared affection. Baby talk and a half-dozen nicknames characterize the conversation between the Egalitarian and his or her dog.

Utilitarians and Egalitarians may share a love for dogs, but never the twain shall meet from that point on. And proselytizing the other side is mostly futile. Utilitarians will never persuade Egalitarians to "just leave the dog in the car" overnight at the motel, and Egalitarians will never convince Utilitarians to "just have him up on the couch." At least they can agree that owning a dog is a worthwhile endeavor, as opposed to those poor souls who can't even see the point. These are the people you come across on your walks who recoil when your dog tries to nicely greet them. What can you do? Some people are just DUDs (Don't Understand Dogs). Onward and upward.

My conversion from semi-Utilitarian to full-blown Egalitarian took place almost immediately after Ben came home. Here I thought I was getting a dog to sniff out game birds during the fall hunting season in the Upper Midwest. Confirming that Utilitarian intention was the outdoor dog run that had been constructed in the side yard in anticipation of Ben's arrival. "Dogs live outside," after all.

At least that is where our family dogs had always lived for as long as I could remember. There was the half-Lab, half-Samoyed, Muffy, whose favored napping location was in the middle of the street, and the two Siberian huskies, Tonka and Tinka, who actually preferred being out in the cold, marauding about in search of smaller animals.

Ben was different, much different. He would never spend a night in that pen. In fact, it was soon dismantled and removed, thus providing the first clue that I had changed. Or rather, that I had *been changed* simply by the presence of a different kind of dog that didn't demand in-house residence but rather just seemed to belong there.

Silly me for thinking that I had simply acquired "a dog." When, in truth, what had been bestowed upon me was a year-round, life-enriching relationship that would expand my boundaries of joy and sorrow, and help me understand poignant lessons about life and faith.

This is the story of my boy, Ben. It's a story about love and loss. But most especially, it's a story about grace.

CHAPTER 1

DESIRING A DOG, IN A DISTANT LAND

"Fish out of water" would be the apt description. It was spring, and I was in a hotel room in Tokyo, feeling a million miles away from home.

Mind you, I was used to international travel, having competed in tennis tournaments all over the world on the professional tennis tour for the previous ten years. London, Paris, Melbourne, Moscow, Hong Kong . . . you name the city, I had probably been there.

But Tokyo? I had visited this megalopolis many times previously, but could never get past the sense that I had somehow touched down on a completely different planet.

Here I was, a midwestern boy who was used to the land and life of Lake Minnetonka, Minnesota, an All-American, Norman Rockwell-like suburb of Minneapolis, dropping in on a place and pace that left me disoriented at every turn.

The traffic? "Jam!" as the taxi driver in his broken English would call it. The skyline? An erector set gone stark raving mad. The air quality? Now you know why they wear those white masks. The food? Unrecognizable and expensive. The language? Spoken or written, good luck.

This is not to say that Japan is without merit. The people are respectful, the landscapes beautiful . . . once you get outside the erector set.

The cherry blossoms may have been in bloom that spring, but my spirits weren't. I wanted out of Tokyo, and I wanted something else — a yellow Lab. While the former looked promising (the tournament would last only a week), the latter seemed as many miles away as I was from home.

I had arrived in Tokyo resigned to the fact that I wasn't getting a dog anytime soon. Being single and spending nine months of the year on the road was not a recipe for conscientious dog ownership. At this stage of my life, I would need lots of help to have a dog — like a weeks-on-end dog-sitter. But who could possibly love me that much?

"Hello, Mom and Dad! I was just thinking that if you could take care of . . ."

Unfortunately, they weren't biting.

My mother had dogs all of her life and didn't want the responsibility that went with it anymore. She had a springer in her childhood, a chow as a wedding gift, the Lab/Samoyed mix, Muffy, while raising my three older siblings, and then the rampaging, shedding, hole-digging Siberian huskies while I grew up. My mom loved her dogs, but she was nearing seventy and well beyond giving in to the-kids-want-a-dog-but-you-know-who-will-take-care-of-it routine.

My father agreed. Not only did he not want to take care of my dog when I was out of town, but he specifically didn't want a Lab, for one reason — and I quote him precisely, "Because their tails knock stuff off the coffee table." Turns out he had seen his friend's Lab do this very thing way back when, and — whoa — had it made an impression. There was no changing his mind on this one.

So this is what I was up against. For the past few months I had tried every persuasive angle (as only the youngest child knows how to employ), but to no avail. It was just, "David, we're fine with your getting a dog, but we're not taking care of it when you're gone."

This was not difficult to translate. It was like saying to your sixteen-year-old son who doesn't have two nickels to rub together, "We're fine with your getting a brand new sports car; we're just not going to pay for it." In other words, it ain't happening.

So there I was, alone in Tokyo, finally coming to the realization that a yellow Labrador puppy wasn't going to be in my foreseeable future. And I'll admit it—this was tough to swallow. I wasn't so much upset at my folks as I was with the futility of my situation. My parents were doing what parents are supposed to do—be realistic and make responsible decisions. As for me, I was out of viable options. What was I going to do, quit my tennis career so that I could get a dog? I may have been in my carefree twenties, but I still had a little bit of sense.

Why did I want a dog so badly anyway? It wasn't like I had never had one before. I could even relate to my parents' lament, "We have had enough dogs to know that we have had enough of dogs." And besides, any relationship with a dog at this point in my life was going to be most definitely long distance—without the phone calls, without the letters . . . without much of anything, now that I think of it.

So what was motivating me? Okay, I'll be honest; there was one reason I wanted a dog, and that was to find, flush, and fetch pheasants.

Which, in and of itself, is quite ironic.

I grew up in a family without a single hunting or fishing gene.

3

My grandfather did neither, my dad had no interest, and not surprisingly, my older siblings followed suit. We may have lived on a great fishing lake in a state with all kinds of outdoor opportunities, but sports—tennis, ice hockey, and skiing—were our recreational activities, not pursuing wild game. In fact, until my mid-twenties, I'm not sure I could have even identified a pheasant if it had crossed the road in front of me.

And me actually shoot a bird? Not a chance. I may have known nothing about hunting while growing up, but I did know this: I was not going to be a hunter. As a boy, I remember driving through Wisconsin during hunting season on our way to a tennis tournament in Chicago and being repulsed, even outraged, by the dead deer I saw strapped to the roof of every fourth car. I even felt bad for the fish whenever I saw one get caught by an angler trolling by our family's shoreline. I may have liked hamburgers as much as the next kid, but any hunting for me would take place at Wendy's and not in the great outdoors.

What I never anticipated is that two interests of my youth would combine years later and turn me into a pheasant hunter. And what were those two interests? Dogs and guns.

I've told you something about the dog part, how dogs were a regular part of our family throughout my childhood. I was not only the youngest child, but nearly nine years behind my next-oldest sibling, leaving me to be the only child at home by the time I was in the fourth grade. Without any siblings around, Tonka and Tinka, the Siberian huskies, became my constant companions.

Even my most memorable Christmas had to do with dogs. That was when I was about ten, and after we had finished opening gifts, my parents informed me that they had "one more special present" (something, I might add, every child wants to hear). They told me to look out the front window, and what should my wide eyes behold in the snow-covered yard but a handmade, wood dogsled glistening in the sun. I thought I had died and gone to the Iditarod! For many a winter thereafter, I fondly remember harnessing up the huskies, jumping on the back of that sled, and yelling, "Mush!" Off across the frozen lake we'd go, with no particular destination in mind—just a kid loving life with his dogs.

So dogs were always there. And so were guns, albeit to a lesser extent. I distinctly recall tagging along and watching my dad and older brothers shoot a .22 rifle or shotgun, and how much of an indelible mark that made on me. Even shooting my dad's BB gun around the yard at a dock post or a tree was something I just plain liked to do. Don't get me wrong—we weren't some militia family with an armory of weapons stored in the cellar. Far from it. But in my youth, I was exposed enough to shooting to realize I liked pulling that trigger.

Growing up, I may have loved dogs and loved shooting, but combining them to become a pheasant hunter wouldn't happen until my mid-twenties because of another, even greater all-consuming pursuit—tennis.

I hit my first tennis balls with a sawed-off wood racquet when I was just four, played my first tournament at eight, won the Minnesota State High School tennis title in ninth grade, moved to Florida at fifteen to train at the famous Nick Bollettieri Tennis Academy, went to Stanford on a tennis scholarship, turned pro at nineteen, and by my early twenties, was ranked number twelve in the world.

Did I mention that tennis was all-consuming?

As a pro, my life was like this: wake up, eat breakfast, practice two hours in the morning, have lunch, play a practice match in the afternoon, lift weights, do agility drills and cardiovascular conditioning, eat dinner, and go to bed. Next day: repeat.

Then I'd be off to the airport for an eighteen-hour flight to Australia or some other faraway place where I'd . . . wake up, eat breakfast, practice, play a match, eat dinner, and go to bed at the hotel. Next day: repeat. Next week: fly to another city for another tournament to do it all over again.

You can probably imagine how anything that took this much commitment, energy, and focus eventually altered my conception of "playing tennis" into "working tennis."

Like any job, there were the good parts and the bad parts. The good parts were competing at big tournaments like Wimbledon and the U.S. Open, experiencing new places and people, and making a very good living doing it. The bad parts were the long flights, the jet lag, the injuries, the tedium. Losing in the first round wasn't very much fun either.

Ever since my mid-teens when I jumped on this fast-moving tennis treadmill, I found myself instinctively seeking relief from the grind. There was the surfing phase in high school, which saw me driving to the beach every spare moment. There were the girlfriends in college and during my early twenties. There was the constant hankering to go home to Minnesota to be with family, to play ice hockey, to go out on the lake . . . to do *anything* to take a break from the airport-to-hotel-to-tennis-courts monotony.

So maybe it shouldn't have come as such a shock that I would eventually rediscover my love for dogs and guns, triggered (pardon the pun) by a most unusual person in a most unlikely place.

* * *

There I was in a windowless weightlifting room surrounded by bars and bells and benches in the underground bowels of an indoor racquet and fitness club in Minneapolis. My fitness coach Sol, who held the same position with the Minnesota Timberwolves NBA team, was putting me through another grueling workout—squats, lunges, calf raises, abs—a regimen that, on many occasions, left me barely able to walk.

This was familiar turf for us. We spent countless hours in that weight room, pumping iron and bantering between sets about anything and everything—life, sports, the guy across the room with the terrible form. You know, important stuff like that.

Sol's personal background was the most interesting topic of all. His parents had survived Nazi prison camps during World War II, immigrated to Israel in the late 1940s, and then brought Sol and his older brother to America in the 1950s.

Coming from such divergent backgrounds, we were surprised to discover one day that we had two interests in common that had gone dormant in both of our lives. You guessed it—dogs and guns.

Like me, Sol grew up with dogs, and now with his parents becoming older and infirm, he began to take care of their big golden retriever named Chip. Unlike me though, Sol was an outdoorsman. He was an avid fisherman and former hunter, having given up the latter twenty years earlier when he felt bad after shooting, of all things, a red squirrel. That was it—no more hunting for him.

One conversation led to another, and the next thing I knew, we were driving out to a friend's forty-acre tract of land just outside the suburban limits of Minneapolis with a .22 rifle in the back of the car. It was fun to hear the crack of a rifle again after all those years and see the steel spinner target twirl. We would finish our weightlifting workout at 5:00 p.m. and rush out there just in time to get a half-hour of plinking in before dark. Depth of snow and degree of temp did not matter—Sol was in the NBA's traveling circus, I was on the tennis tour's traveling road show, and we both needed some relief.

We soon desired a new shooting challenge and found it in the form of flying clay targets. This necessitated graduation from a .22, which fires a single bullet, to a shotgun, which shoots a cluster of tiny BBs, thus increasing the odds of breaking the flying four-inch clay discs. With eye-hand coordination developed over years of hitting a moving yellow ball, this was right up my alley.

All this shooting was rekindling the hunting gene in Sol to the point that he arranged a half-day pheasant hunt at a local outdoor club. He invited a couple old friends to join him. And yes, he also invited me.

I remember pondering whether I should go. I certainly didn't want to shoot a pheasant. So why would I go pheasant hunting? Sort of defeats the purpose, right? But there I was that Saturday morning, twenty-six years old, standing beside Sol's truck on the edge of a large field of knee-high grass holding a double-barreled shotgun I had borrowed from my brother—a gun that he had nicknamed "Old Betsy"—and wondering, *Now what?*

With my graduation from rifle to shotgun, from stationary target to moving, and now from shooting range to hunting field, serendipity was about to occur. Or, as the dictionary defines it, "the faculty of making fortunate discoveries by accident." Only it didn't take any of my faculties to make this fortunate discovery. Serendipity was about to jump out of the back of Sol's friend's pickup truck with four legs and a wagging tail.

There were actually three dogs that day running underfoot around our parked vehicles, sniffing each other, and generally looking very excited about what was to take place. Sol's friend Mike had a scruffy half-springer spaniel, half-golden retriever named Zach; Sol's other friend Randy had a black Lab named Cinders; and Sol had his parent's dog Chip, a purebred golden retriever.

Having never seen a hunting dog in action, I remember trying to envision what these dogs were actually going to do. They looked like regular family pets to me, the kind that basically eat and sleep their way through life just like the dogs we'd always had. I figured they were there for aesthetic purposes, or worse, that they would be running wild, sort of like my Siberian huskies when they chased after some smaller mammal.

Imaginings ended, the four of us formed a line with about ten yards of space between each hunter, which to me looked like something you'd see on the evening news when a search party makes its way through a field looking for a missing person. Apparently we were going to do the same—march back and forth in a line around this big field in search of pheasants that were purportedly hiding in the grass. Pheasants? I didn't see any pheasants.

In formation and ready to set out, I looked down the line and noticed that the springer-golden mix, Zach, and the black Lab, Cinders, were hovering with anticipation around the feet of their respective owners. In fact, Zach was standing right in front of Mike looking straight up into his eyes with a locked gaze and quivering tail. This was in sharp contrast to Sol's golden, who seemed as unaware of what was about to take place as I was.

Have you ever been in a real-life situation and you felt like a movie was taking place around you? Well, that is exactly how I felt for the next two hours. The "movie" started when Mike looked down at his dog and said three simple words, "Hunt 'em up."

As if on remote control, Zach immediately turned around, darted fifteen yards in front of Mike, and starting running in tight figure-eight patterns as if in search of something in the thick grass.

Wow, I thought, *it's almost like that dog knows what he's doing.*

Within minutes, that hunch was confirmed. The scruffy dog became even more intense with his gait quickening, ears perking, and his tail going a million miles an hour. Duly warned by this obvious change in his behavior, I was still utterly surprised when a huge pheasant burst up out of the grass right in front of Zach's nose in a loud flurry of flapping wings. In fact, I was too stunned to raise my gun for a shot. The sequence of watching the dog zero in and then flush up this unseen bird from the grass had left me temporarily paralyzed.

Mike showed no such inaction. Quickly raising his shotgun, he pulled the trigger and with one BANG dropped the pheasant about thirty yards in front of us. Zach ran to the spot in a flash, scooped up the bird in his mouth, and proudly carried his prize back to Mike, delivering it into his hand. I stood there in open-mouthed amazement as Mike tucked the bird into the rear pouch of his hunting vest.

I'm pretty sure I became a pheasant hunter right then . . . without even firing a shot.

Reorganizing ourselves back into a line, we realized that Chip, Sol's golden, had suddenly gone missing. We looked and called and whistled but to no avail. So we all made a U-turn back toward the vehicles where, lo and behold, there was Chip . . . underneath Sol's truck. As I said, there were three dogs there that day—two were hunting dogs and the other entered retirement after his first ten minutes afield. This old dog was not about to learn new tricks—Chip was gun-shy.

Sol put Chip inside the truck and we headed back into the grass with Zach and Cinders working like a pair of vacuums, nosing every nook and cranny of the field. The same scenario repeated itself time and again—dog gets "birdy," dog flushes bird, Mike or

Randy shoots bird, and dog returns bird to his hand. The pheasants that got away were the ones Sol and I shot at. We quickly found out that breaking clay targets was one thing, bagging a pheasant, quite another.

The movie came to a close two hours later as we convened around the back of Mike's pickup truck. The dogs lapped up water while the guys recounted the hunt. Somehow, eight dead pheasants lying on the tailgate didn't elicit my former repugnance to hunting. In fact, this first time afield gave me a broader perspective on the food chain. Heretofore, I had been a consumer, operating under the premise that poultry was to be found in the meat section of the supermarket—headless, de-feathered, and under plastic wrap. Now, with my first experience as a hunter, I gained a whole new understanding, appreciation, respect, even a sense of personal responsibility for the process of putting food on the table, from field to family.

I was also mesmerized by the amazing bond and teamwork between man and dog that I had just witnessed. A human duo couldn't have done this dance. But man and dog could, and it was a beautiful thing to behold. Each was dependent on the other. Without the man, the dog could find and flush a bird but would never be able to retrieve one. Without the dog, the man would walk through the field not finding, flushing, or taking home much of anything.

I found this out the frustrating way over the next two autumns. A few friends and I would make Saturday jaunts out to farm country, traipse around a field all day, and go home with *maybe* one pheasant amongst the four of us. And that was on a good day. I knew what was missing—a hunting dog. But the prospects of getting one anytime soon seemed all too remote.

That began to change late one afternoon on a drive home from

11

yet another fruitless hunt. We stopped my Jeep atop a gravel road that overlooked a large, dried-out marsh in the Minnesota River Valley. It was a stunning fall scene. The air was still and fresh and the color of the marsh and surrounding trees unusually brilliant as the setting sun cast a "Wow is that for real?" glow across the landscape and sky. We looked down to see two men in the middle of the marsh, separated by about fifteen yards, walking very deliberately away from us, almost as if they were measuring every step. The men, with shotguns in hand, were intently focused on their two black Labs quartering back and forth through the reeds in front of them.

I lowered the windows and turned off the engine. We were all struck by the quietness outside. The hunters and dogs were well over a football field away, and yet the sound of the dogs bounding through the dry marsh carried easily to us. We soaked in this live painting for about five minutes, maybe ten. Nothing happened—no pheasants were flushed, no shots were fired, no retrieves were made by the dogs. It was just a beautiful scene that subconsciously flipped a switch in my head to the I-must-get-a-dog position. We drove off, and my search for a dog officially began.

* * *

The first question I had to consider was, *What kind of dog?* If you've ever watched the Westminster Kennel Club Dog Show, which takes place every February at Madison Square Garden in New York City, you know how many different breeds there are. In fact, there are so many breeds (nearly two hundred) that they are divided into seven groups: herding, hound, working, terrier, sporting, non-sporting, and last but not least, the ever-popular toy group. Wanting a dog that could carry a pheasant rather than the other way around, I quickly eliminated the toy group and narrowed my focus to the sporting group, which includes breeds that historically have been bred and used for hunting birds on land and over water. These are the various and sundry kinds of retrievers, spaniels, setters, and pointers.

But even within the sporting group there are nearly thirty breeds, all with different looks and traits. Some have long hair, others short. Some are large and leggy, others more compact. Some have the reputation of being high-strung ("energetic and need exercise," as the announcer would diplomatically describe them). Others were "one-person dogs" (translation: suspicious of everyone except their owners).

They are all hunting dogs, but the fundamental distinction is how they go about doing it. The "flushing" breeds, like the Labrador and golden retriever or the springer and cocker spaniel, sniff out a bird and then immediately flush or "spring" the bird into flight. The "pointing" breeds, on the other hand, like the English pointer and the German shorthair pointer, or the English and Irish setter, are equally proficient at finding birds, but instead of moving in to flush them into flight, these dogs are bred to freeze (known as pointing or setting), so the hunter has time to get up close to the dog in order to flush the birds.

Flushing a bird versus pointing a bird may sound like a minor difference, but it's actually the fork in the road for choosing a hunting dog because it affects everything after it: how your dog will be trained, what and where you will hunt, even who you'll hunt with.

So which are better, flushers or pointers? Let's just say this is a matter of personal preference and a particularly touchy question to pose in the company of serious dog people. Everyone has an opinion, and it usually reflects the type of breed they own.

Imagine that.

I came to see the flusher-versus-pointer question as a choice between a sport utility vehicle and a sports car. Each provides transportation, but in vastly different ways. Some prefer the flexibility and practicality of an SUV (i.e., a flushing dog) while others like the performance and style of a sports car (i.e., a pointing dog). And just like your choice between an SUV and a sports car will determine how and where you drive, so will your choice of a flushing or pointing dog determine how and where you hunt.

Having never owned any of these breeds, I researched everything I could find to discover which one would be best for me. I lived in Minnesota, so I needed a dog that could handle cold weather. And though my main interest was hunting pheasants, I thought I might also hunt ducks someday, which would require a dog that liked to swim and retrieve. All the while I was trying to factor in the temperament of the breed. I wanted a dog that I could manage rather than one who would manage me.

After much reading and deliberation, I arrived at a breed that fit the bill, but one that no one had ever heard of—the wirehaired pointing griffon. They point birds that live on land, like pheasants, and unlike most other pointing breeds, they are adept in the water at retrieving ducks. Plus, they have a thick coat that can handle the cold, and are reported to have a mild disposition. I concluded that I had found the perfect crossover between an SUV and a sports car . . . until I saw a picture of one. At the risk of offending the four wirehaired pointing griffon owners who will read this book, they aren't the most attractive dogs in the world. Putting an end to this option was my parents informing me that they wouldn't have such a creature in their home.

Not to be disheartened, I quickly moved on to another breed that sounded intriguing but also something of an oxymoron:

the pointing Lab. Labrador retrievers have the All-American, all-purpose dog reputation. They are the consummate flushing dog—great at retrieving ducks in the water (or a ball for the kids), and yet very proficient at finding, flushing, and retrieving birds on land. They are generally good-natured and quite low maintenance with their short, almost self-cleaning coat. *Perfect*, I thought, *good in the field and with the family*. I could see why Labs are the most popular breed in America.

But that was just the problem. When I read about the most popular breed part, the next sentence was usually about over-breeding and health problems. I questioned whether I could find a good Lab.

And what kind of Lab points, anyway? Yet website after website of pointing Lab breeders from Colorado to Ohio proclaimed with words and pictures that I could "have it all"—a dog who points, retrieves, and swims.

My mind was beginning to swim. Here I thought the fundamental decision was going to be between a flushing dog and a pointing dog; and now the flushing dogs are pointing and the pointing dogs are swimming and retrieving. Meanwhile, I was contemplating whether a pointing Lab would knock stuff off the coffee table or just stare at it.

I had become more confused than ever. And I was going back on the road soon, still with no solution to the "minor detail" about who would take care of my dog when I was away from home.

I may have waded deep into finding the perfect dog, but my parents hadn't moved from square one, "We don't want to be responsible for your dog." Despite lots of pleading, they weren't budging.

So there I was in that tiny hotel room in Tokyo, a million miles from home and coming to grips with the fact that I wasn't getting a dog anytime soon. The vision had faded. Research would stop. It was over. The End.

And then I saw a fax slide under the door of my hotel room.

CHAPTER 2

AND ON THE THIRD DAY,
A DOWN PAYMENT

A fax under my hotel room door was not an unusual occurrence. In fact, I received one almost every day on the road from my dear mother bringing news and encouragement from home. It's hard to imagine now, but this was before email, texting, tweets, and smart phones had become a regular part of life.

The arrival of a fax may have been typical, but this day was not. It was Good Friday, and a bright and sunny one in Tokyo. I snapped up the pages from the floor, sprawled out on my bed, and with the sun shining through the window, I started to read.

My mother is a stream-of-consciousness writer. Factual brevity is not her style. The thoughts flow and the words multiply, often totaling four or more pages. There is some reporting but far more editorializing—and lots of repetition. Everything is personal, from and to the heart. Reminders, admonitions, and life lessons are woven throughout. Bible verses will be in one paragraph, a tennis tip or two in the next.

From the start, it was clear (as it always is) what this fax was about . . . and yet it didn't make much sense. She was going on and on about this beautiful Lab she had seen on her daily walk through the neighborhood. Yogi was his name. Turns out Yogi's owner, Tom, lived only a few blocks away, but for some reason my mom had "never seen Yogi before."

I quote her words because there's a little interpretation to be done here. Yogi was more than a year old at the time. My mother walked every day in the neighborhood right by Yogi's house. The chance of my mother never having seen Yogi in over a year of walks is minuscule at best. The reality was that she had never *noticed* Yogi before. An important distinction, because something had obviously caused my mother to notice Yogi for the first time and then write to me all about it from across the ocean. Why was she so interested in this dog all of a sudden?

In typical fashion, every last detail about Yogi was described— his beautiful white coat, the big brown eyes, his proportioned build ("not like one of those skinny salamander Labs"), his friendly personality. Having never thought of a question she didn't eventually ask, I can only imagine the twenty-question . . . er, hundred-question routine Tom must have fielded when my mom came across the two of them on the street.

Of course, the "Where did you get him?" query was posed, and it turned out that Tom had watched—surprise, surprise—the Westminster Dog Show and looked up the breeder who won "Best of Breed" for Labradors. Conveniently enough, the breeder lived only a few hours' drive to the south in Iowa. It wasn't long before single-guy Tom had sidekick Yogi . . . and was loving him to pieces.

I practically gobbled up the letter, savoring every word, what with dogs firmly planted on my brain for the last several months. And then near the end of the fax, as if to leave me tantalized in Tokyo, my mom dropped this little sentence, "If I ever got a Lab, I'd want to get one just like that."

What did she just say?! "If I ever got a Lab"? My mom had

never given me the slightest notion that she would even consider getting another dog, let alone a Lab. And now she says, "If I ever got a Lab, I'd want to get one just like that"?

This was hope—pure unadulterated hope—that left my eyes darting around the ceiling and my imagination drifting to places in the country, in the woods, on the lake where I would venture with a dog. Someone else may have read this sentence and been tempered by the "if" part. But I knew better because *I knew* my mother. She wouldn't go into such great detail and be so complimentary about this dog if something hadn't changed in her mind. I concluded that if she was talking about a Lab, she must be thinking about getting one!

Finishing the rest of the fax, I went off to tennis practice that day with a little extra spring in my step.

The next morning was Saturday, and I awoke to find another fax from home under the door. I dove right in, hoping for a morsel or two about Yogi or anything to do with dogs. I got much more than that. Turned out my mother had called Yogi's breeder, a woman named Donna Reece, who owned Ridge View Labradors in northeast Iowa. The conversation lasted two hours, and my mother had scribbled down several pages of notes. Donna explained her philosophy of breeding Labs to have "soft" dispositions with the proper show conformation while also retaining the natural hunting instincts of the breed.

Often, Lab breeders focus on producing show stock or hunting stock . . . but not both. The result can be pretty dogs that don't have much hunting drive or Labs that don't look much like Labs but hunt like crazy. But Donna Reece? Apparently she was on a mission to produce the perfect all-around Lab.

My mom went on and on about how much she had learned from Donna. Shortly after finishing the fax, I boarded the bus to go to the tennis center. Or perhaps I should say my body boarded the bus, because my mind was miles away—wondering, speculating, and above all, hoping.

* * *

The light shone brightly around the edges of my hotel room curtains the following morning. It was Easter Sunday, but it certainly didn't feel like it. I wouldn't be going to church to celebrate the resurrection, and there wouldn't be a meal with family and friends afterward. Today would be another day at the tennis center. The professional tennis show must go on—even on Easter Sunday.

Before the show started though, there was another fax to read. I wish I could remember more of what was written, but the stunning announcement in the first paragraph overwhelmed everything else, "I called Donna back and sent her a down payment on a puppy."

What?! Three days ago my mother wasn't interested in getting a dog. Two days ago, she saw a nice Lab while on a walk. Yesterday, she talked with the breeder. And today she plunked down a couple hundred dollars on a puppy . . . a puppy, incidentally, that hadn't even been *conceived* yet?

This was just so completely out of character for my mother to make such a quick decision, because she was the farthest thing from impulsive. For her, a child of the Great Depression, to mail a two-hundred-dollar check to a person she had never met who lived in another state for a dog that hadn't even been born? Pigs fly.

The rest of the fax filled in the details: Donna was planning a breeding in a couple weeks between Gus, one of her original dogs, and Icy, the daughter of her prized breeding female, Snobear.

The puppies were to be born in late June and ready to be picked up in mid-August.

I wish I could report that all this good news from home inspired me to swashbuckle my way through the tournament and mow down all who came into my path. But that wasn't the case. I lost in the early rounds and was on a flight home shortly thereafter with the urgency of a horse returning to the stables. No, there wouldn't be a puppy waiting for me when I landed, but at least I could now see the light at the end of a very long tunnel.

* * *

Disoriented would be a good way to describe how I felt as my folks and I drove through southern Minnesota on the way to see Donna in Iowa just two days after I arrived home from Tokyo. Having gone from that urban erector set in the Far East, to gazing out the window at rural landscapes of rolling hills and unplanted fields — and the occasional Amish horse and buggy — in a span of forty-eight hours, was hard to process.

Making our way through small farm communities in northeast Iowa, we finally arrived in Elkader, a quaint town situated just twenty miles west of the mighty Mississippi. A couple turns through the main streets took us to the outskirts where the road changed from pavement to gravel, and then, with no fanfare to announce its presence, there it was — Ridge View Labradors. The place I had been hearing about half a world away consisted of Donna's modest-sized country rambler and a small kennel building across the driveway that housed about twenty dogs, all of whom started barking as we turned in.

Within moments of meeting Donna, I could tell she was one of those take-no-thought-for-self dog people. The vast majority of her time, energy, and thought centered on her dogs, not furnishings, landscaping, clothes, and other mundanities of life. This is not to say she dressed or decorated poorly; it's just that she personified the sign over the kitchen: "This house is for Labrador retrievers. If you don't like it, you can leave."

We were soon introduced to Snobear, the top-producing female Labrador in AKC history. Not surprisingly, she ruled the house with the air of a queen. Right beside Snobear was her daughter Icy, who played the princess role well.

We then went outside to the kennel to see Donna's other dogs. All of her Labs were beautiful. While she had a few black Labs and one or two chocolates, most were of the yellow variety, either in a honey or ivory hue. Each dog had its distinctive look, yet their abundant similarities communicated "same family." It was the pleasant faces, the almond-shaped eyes, the proportioned builds, the straight coats and otter tails, and that soft disposition that I had heard so much about. These dogs were sweet, inside and out.

The one dog we hadn't seen yet was Ben's father-to-be, Gus—or as his official name read, Gust o' Wind. Gus lived with Donna's parents a mile or so up the road, so we hopped into the car to see our future puppy's sire. We were immediately impressed— actually taken aback—by Gus. And not because he looked like another "Donna dog." In fact, Gus looked less Westminster and more *Winchester*, as in the kind of traditional American hunting Lab you see pictured on the cover of the Winchester firearms catalog, soaking wet with muscled haunches, sitting beside his master in a marsh-side blind, scanning the sky with a focused gaze for the next raft of ducks to appear.

Gus had gravitas. His bearing was so serious that baby-talking to him would have been totally out of the question. "Good day, sir" seemed far more appropriate than "Hey, sweetie!" for this eighty-five pound specimen. The dog exuded weightiness . . . and I don't mean in pounds.

The day was getting on, so we drove back to Donna's to say our thank-yous and good-byes. Donna's father followed in his own vehicle with Gus and asked me if I'd like to see Gus do a few minutes of "practice hunting" before we headed home. Having been impressed by Gus and hoping my future puppy would get a little bit of him, I willingly agreed. So Donna's dad and I crossed the gravel road to a strip of trees and grass between two cornfields.

We walked west. I know that because the setting sun was casting an orange glow over the sky in front of us. All was quiet except for the sound of feet and paws moving through the grass. "Hunt 'em up," Donna's father said calmly to Gus, as if speaking to another human being. I watched as Gus muscled through the grass with complete purpose and amazing athleticism.

I thought back on all that had happened in the past week, from urban Tokyo to rural Iowa. Something bigger was going on here, something far beyond what I—or my mother or Donna Reece—could have orchestrated. The confluence of events that brought us to this place at this time and the breeding that was about to occur two weeks hence could not have been random.

My mother wanted a nice-looking Lab with a soft disposition—like Yogi. I wanted all of that, plus a little hunt in the genes—like Gus. Even before meeting us, Donna had already planned to breed Yogi's mother, Icy, with Gus, this stud of a dog that my eyes were fixated on in front of me. On paper, this was a perfect match for us—Westminster and Winchester rolled into one.

Put it all together and one might conclude that the stars had aligned, the fates were smiling, good luck was ours. At the time, I didn't give it much thought—I was just happy to be getting a puppy. But looking back at these early days and then forward through the life-altering experience of having Ben, it would become clear that it was actually divine providence at work every step of the way.

In fact, providence *is* the story of Ben . . . from preconception, to puppyhood, to adulthood, to his passing, to the grace that would follow—the story of how God can use even a dog to bless and teach and guide the course of a life. Or in this case, several lives.

It was way too early for me to comprehend all that as we drove home that night. Looking out the window into the darkness, I did know that something felt very good and very right about all this. Things were definitely looking up.

Or perhaps better said, God was looking down.

CHAPTER 3

WHO CHOSE WHOM?

Arriving home after having just seen the breeder and "parents" of my future puppy, I immediately began to take on the fidgetiness of a first-time father, as in, *I'm going to be a dad! Now what do I do?!*

I figured I'd better be prepared for the arrival of this little bundle of joy, so I did exactly what any half-panicked father-to-be would do: read a how-to book on dog training.

My fitness coach Sol, now with a black Lab of his own, recommended that I get one of the classic books by the legendary dog training author Richard Wolters. I had never heard of Wolters, but quickly discerned that his reputation for being able to take the research of animal behaviorists and make it understandable, applicable, and even humorous for the average dog owner would make him the right guy for me. First he wrote *Gun Dog*, then *Water Dog*, then *Family Dog*, then *Game Dog*, then *City Dog*, then *Kid's Dog*, then . . . well, you get the picture. He even wrote a masterpiece on Labs entitled *The Labrador Retriever: The History . . . the People.*

If you squint a little at Wolters' picture, you might think he's related to Doc, the disheveled, white-haired mad scientist with the time-machine sports car from the 1980s hit movie *Back to the Future*. Wolters, who died in the early 1990s, was about as eccentric too, with his passions spanning the spectrum of atomic science, fine arts, photography, and yes, dog training.

I chose his book *Game Dog* because the subtitle—*The Hunter's Retriever for Upland Birds and Waterfowl*—precisely stated what I desired in a dog. I dove right into the book as if it were my first meal after a week-long fast. Mind you, I was coming off a kind of lifetime fast when it came to dog training. Sure, I had plenty of experience with our past family dogs. But me actually *read* a book on dog training or take a puppy to obedience school? That Rubicon had never been crossed.

This, of course, is one of the classic characteristics of Utilitarian dog owners. Back in my Utilitarian days, I knew dogs could be trained, but I was woefully unaware of the diligent step-by-step teaching and reinforcing process that is required to do so. I figured if I wanted the dog to "come," I'd just say the word . . . then again . . . and again. And if the dog was still ignoring me, I raised my voice and called in a more menacing tone. If that failed, I moved on to my ace-in-the-hole, which was, "Tonka want a treat?!" This dalliance with his stomach usually caused him to stop what he was doing and enthusiastically run over to me, but deep down I knew I was being used. No matter, if he came, I considered him "trained."

To be fair, not all Utilitarians are as lacking as I was when it comes to training their own dogs. Some just don't have the time or patience. So they send their dogs off to an expert for two or three months of training and boarding at Doggy Finishing School and receive back a lower risk of embarrassment at the end of the term. Egalitarians, don't smirk—you've dreamed about doing this with your kids.

Reading *Game Dog* was a major catalyst in pushing me further over to the Egalitarian side of the dog owner scale. Dripping off the pages of Wolters' book was the close companionship he had with his dogs. His training involved lots of time and communication—two cornerstones of any good relationship. This led to Wolters' viewing his dogs not merely as dogs but rather as friends, teammates, family members. Losing one crushed him. That drew me in.

After devouring Wolters' book, I couldn't wait to put all my learning into practice. But how was I going to do that? I wouldn't have my own dog for months. A thought popped into my head. *What about training someone else's dog? What about . . . Yogi?*

And so there I was with Yogi down at the park every day teaching him "sit," "stay," and "come," and throwing one of those retrieving dummies for him that was shaped like an extra-large cucumber. Yogi took to it all pretty well too, despite the fact that he was a goofball and well over a year old, way past the optimal age that Wolters recommended—no, *demanded*—that one starts training a dog.

After six weeks at home experimenting on Yogi, the time came for me to get back on the road to play tennis. So in early June, having learned that Icy was pregnant after breeding with Gus, I flew to London to get ready for Wimbledon. "The Championships," as Wimbledon is sometimes called, is the game's premier tournament and is played on the picture-perfect lawns of the historic All England Club just outside London. I packed all my usual assortment of tennis clothes and shoes for the trip . . . along with *Game Dog* neatly inserted between the six racquets in my carry-on bag.

For the past several months, I had been nursing a chronic elbow injury, causing my game to be a little rusty upon touching down across the Atlantic. Making matters worse, the damp and cool weather so common in England made the tennis ball feel about as soggy as the one your dog drops at your feet. In a matter of days, my elbow was throbbing, and I soon found myself in a doctor's office on the wrong end of a long needle for yet another cortisone injection. This is not what I would call ideal preparation for the game's grandest event. Predictably and disappointingly, I lost in the first round.

I took the loss hard. As a boy, I had dreamed of lifting the champion's golden chalice, and now as a man, Wimbledon was my favorite tournament, motivating me to push myself that extra bit further. I had made a run to the semifinals back when I was twenty-two years old, winning a memorable five-set match over Andre Agassi on Centre Court along the way. But now, twenty-nine years old and ten years into my tennis career, I was entering the time when most tennis pros start getting put out to pasture.

Life felt bleak that night as I put my head on the pillow of my rented flat in London. Another Wimbledon had come and gone for me, seemingly before it had even started. The glory days now seemed farther away than ever, and new ones out of the question. I could have used an encouraging word that night, but none was to be found.

What I didn't know was that on that very day, Tuesday, June 23, thousands of miles away from England back in Elkader, Iowa, a very encouraging development was taking place that would give me another type of shot in the arm. Icy had just given birth to six healthy puppies, three males and three females. At the very moment my tennis seemed to be dying, a new part of my life was being born.

I heard about the new litter upon returning to the States. But with a busy summer of tournaments ahead, I would have to focus on more than counting down the weeks to a new puppy.

That was going to be easier said than done. I had already read the early chapter in Wolters' book about picking a puppy, but now I began to give more serious thought to his advice. Being slightly on the analytical and perfectionistic side (okay, a lot), it wasn't enough for me to be getting a great puppy from a great breeder. I wanted to get just the *right* puppy.

Egalitarians expend plenty of brain bytes about this type of thing because "each puppy has its own distinct personality," and therefore "you must choose the right one for you." Utilitarians, on the other hand, are just as apt to take a quick look at the litter, conclude that one is as good as the next, and off they go, pup in hand (correction: pup in crate).

Fortunately, I would be spared the agony of too many options because my parents and I had decided to get a male, thereby eliminating half the litter. Someone had told us the Lab legend that "males are more affectionate," and that was enough to convince us. Of course, this was totally subjective . . . but we were going with it.

Wolters didn't traffic in any of these male-versus-female myths (another one being "females are better hunters"), but he did stress the importance of discerning the pecking order that is established early on in the puppy pack and avoiding the two extremes: the Big Boss puppy who pushes all others aside on his way to the front of the dish, and the Wallflower puppy who gets stepped on by the rest of the litter. Wolters advised getting a middle-of-the-pack puppy purely for trainability reasons, as Big Boss would need an equally strong-willed owner, while the Wallflower was more apt to wilt under the lightest training regimen.

To figure out how the puppies had been imprinted, he recommended taking each one to a place away from its littermates to perform the Campbell puppy behavior tests, such as holding the puppy a few inches off the ground or putting him on his back to see how much he resists. The point being that the strong-willed puppy would vehemently squirm, while the weaker puppy would easily give up, as if to say, "Just shoot me." Wolters didn't sell this as the surefire way to pick the perfect puppy, but it was convincing enough that I would try it with each male in Ben's litter.

The reality was that none of us were in a situation to take on the challenge of a "project dog." If the first rule of thumb in finding the right dog is to "know thyself"—your lifestyle, your energy level, your living quarters, your work schedule—we knew ourselves well enough to understand that my parents were too old and I too frequently gone to have any kind of dog other than one that would blend right in rather than mix things up.

We also understood that the initial months of fun and smiles with a puppy are simply the warm-up for ten, maybe fifteen years of life with a dog that, depending on the dog's disposition, would greatly impact our own dispositions, for better or for worse. There would be years of rearing and training, loving and caring, feeding and exercising, paying and praying, and eventually being sick with grief upon seeing him or her go. Whatever we could do at the beginning to increase our chances that the sum and substance of "life with dog" would end up being a positive one, we were all in for that.

This is why Donna Reece was so promising for us. She seemed to have mastered, as we say in tennis, "all the shots"—from selecting which dogs to breed, to whelping her puppies with lots of handling and socialization to achieve their signature soft disposition.

We would be paying a pretty penny for her expertise, mind

you. Donna's puppies were double what we paid for our Siberian huskies way back when. This triggered a mild debate between my dad and me, with him, still a Utilitarian, harboring some consternation over the sticker price. (Utilitarians like getting a "good deal" on a dog.) I, on the other hand, a newly-minted Egalitarian, rationalized away the purchase price, quoting a study I had seen on the Internet which claimed "the initial cost of a puppy is less than 10% of what will be spent on the dog over its lifetime."

Egalitarian propaganda eventually won out.

* * *

Back home again in early August after playing a string of tournaments, I pointed my Jeep south from Minneapolis and drove with my parents to Donna's to see the now six-week-old puppies for the first time. Again, this was prior to the time when emailing pictures became an everyday occurrence, so we had no idea what the pups looked like before we arrived at Donna's.

Driving through the fields of tall corn in Iowa, I wasn't as concerned about what the puppies looked like as I was about something else—that this would be my only opportunity to see the litter. I was scheduled to be in Cincinnati for a tournament the following week, and therefore would not be able to join my parents for final selection and take-home day. All sorts of doubts bounced around in my head. *What if I can't tell much by the behavior tests? What if my parents like a different pup when they come back next week?* I had been waiting for years for this moment, and now all of a sudden I felt pressure to make the right decision in just one visit.

We pulled into Donna's driveway with all the dogs woofing up our arrival. Donna greeted us and immediately started to talk about the litter as she walked us over to the whelping area on the side of her house. We looked down over the short fence and there they were—six plump balls of fur ranging in color from honey to ivory. Their tiny faces were picture-perfect with their brown eyes and black noses set in heavy contrast against light-colored coats. Everything about them just screamed, "Adorable!" "Darling!" "Cute!" One would need to have their pulse checked if they didn't get warm feelings when seeing their little otter tails, pink tongues, and the way they piled on top of each other.

Donna reached in and pulled out the three males one by one, placing them a few feet away on the grass. I was surprised. In the whelping pen they had looked like one big blob of fur, folds, and feet. But now out in the open, they were quite distinct in color and size. Puppy Number 1, as we labeled him, was big and all white. Puppy Number 2 was medium-sized and buff-colored. And Puppy Number 3? Well, something seemed awry with him. He looked similar in size and color to Puppy Number 2, but instead of stumbling around the yard like the other two, he just lay in a heap on the spot where he was put down, whimpering and looking half-dazed and hung-over. *Must be having a rough day*, I thought to myself.

Thinking this could be a just-wakened-from-his-nap situation, I tactfully asked Donna what was wrong with him (without actually saying, "What's wrong with him?"). Donna explained that this little guy (whom my parents and I later nicknamed "The Dud") was behind the rest of the litter in his development and that his progress (or lack thereof) in the next week or two would determine whether he would be sold as a regular puppy or placed with an elderly person who needed a laid-back companion.

Sounded reasonable to me, but in my own mind, I had pretty much decided that unless some sort of complete personality makeover occurred over the next week when my parents came back, "The Dud" would not be my next dog.

After standing there for a while watching the pups, I decided to try the behavior tests on each of them. I gathered up Puppy Number 1 in my arms and carried him over to the edge of the yard away from everyone. This was the big-boned, white-coated boy. First, to get a sense of how strong-willed he was, I held him a few inches off the ground for about ten seconds. He didn't kick or whine and was content just to hang there. I then placed him on the ground and rolled him over onto his back to see how much he'd resist being put into a submissive position. Turned out, not much. This boy was far from being the alpha pup of the litter.

Next, I tested how attached he was to humans by sneaking about fifteen feet away and kneeling down to call him to me. He eagerly lumbered over and stayed close to me as I walked around, suddenly realizing he was out in the big bad world now.

Finally, I did one last test to see what kind of prey drive and retrieving desire he might have. I had brought a little retrieving dummy with some pheasant feathers taped around it, and after teasing him with it, I tossed it a few feet away. He scampered after it, sniffed it, sort of picked it up, and then gave me a look that said, "Now what do I do?" I certainly wasn't expecting a perfect delivery back to my hand. For now, his chasing after it seemed a good enough sign to me.

I then performed the same tests on Puppy Number 2. Interestingly, while he didn't squirm much on the hover-above-the-ground test, this little guy did not like being rolled over onto his back. He wanted out of that position, like right now! I pondered how to interpret these seemingly conflicting results when both tests were meant to evaluate the same thing—how the pup would respond to being under the authority of someone else.

In the attraction-to-humans tests, Pup Number 2 again showed some interesting traits. He came enthusiastically when called, like Number 1, but at the same time, he had a greater curiosity to explore around the edge of the yard for a minute or two before running back to me. *Hmmm . . .* I thought, trying to figure out what all this meant.

What especially stood out was Pup Number 2's retrieving desire. When I tossed that dummy, he chased after it, even to the point of finding and carrying it out of some higher grass where it had disappeared.

Now it was time to test Pup Number 3 . . . if you could call it a test. He still hadn't moved from the spot where he had been put down, and when I picked him up, it was like holding puppy Play-Doh in my hands. I tried to run a few of the tests on him, but his lack of response only helped me in one way—to check him off the list.

Tests done and pictures taken, we continued the conversation inside Donna's living room with Snobear, Icy, and the pups milling about underfoot. While Donna and my parents droned on about all things dog, I sat on the couch closely observing the three puppies. Pup Number 3 was finally ambulatory but spent quite a bit of time whining. Pup Number 1 made his way around the room aimlessly for a while before lying down to sleep in the middle of the floor.

Pup Number 2, however, was quite different. He had a bearing about him that was not like the others. There was a depth, a maturity, as if his head was screwed on tightly, even at six weeks old. He was curious, yes, but not to the point of venturing too far away into another room or getting himself into trouble. He just calmly checked out here and there, and then walked back over to me, lay down, and fell asleep with his little head on my shoe.

While we still had a week to make the final decision, right then and there I knew which puppy I would choose . . . or perhaps, which puppy had chosen me.

CHAPTER 4

PUPPY-PICKING PANIC

"What?! The Dud is no longer . . . a dud?" I couldn't believe what I was hearing. But it figured, just figured.

A week ago, my folks and I had agreed on the drive home from Donna's that we all liked Pup Number 2. Pup Number 3 was wimpy, Pup Number 1 was nice, but everything about Number 2 was just right—as if he had been specially created for our family. It all seemed so cut and dried. Find a good breeder, spend time with the litter, and the right puppy will become apparent. Signed, sealed, and delivered.

I admit I was surprised that it all had gone so smoothly. We're a—how shall I say?—give-and-take bunch, so I was expecting all kinds of contrary opinions, debates, emotional appeals, and changes of mind in the process of choosing a puppy. But no, there was full consensus on selecting Pup Number 2—and this from folks who have much difficulty making decisions.

That is probably why I had been having a too-good-to-be-true feeling for the first few days after arriving in Cincinnati for the tournament. All was quiet on the home front, but I still had a hunch (okay, a *fear*) that my parents would drive back down to Donna's on Wednesday and fall in love with another puppy. And

I would be left a thousand miles away with no say in the matter.

Sure enough, my phone rang in Cincinnati that Wednesday afternoon. I could tell right away by the tone of their voices that my parents were in a semi-panic. Even my dad, the mild-mannered, always-reasonable, left-brained mechanical engineer was unsettled. They had returned for take-home day and everything had changed. The Dud had, in eight days' time, turned into Mr. Fabulous. Apparently he was playful and bright and cute, nothing like the puppy we had seen the week before. And Big White Boy Number 1 was as adorable as ever.

Everything had changed—that is, except for Pup Number 2. He was as consistent in look and personality as before. He still had the proportioned build, the serious and intelligent bearing.

"So what's the problem?" I asked, feeling as if I were a crisis negotiator trying to talk someone down from the edge of a cliff. "We all liked Number 2 last week and he's the same this week, so let's go with him."

My parents were going to need more convincing than that. They were looking at three wonderful puppies, and I was three states away frantically pacing back and forth in my room. What was I supposed to say, "Don't believe your eyes?" They kept going on and on about each puppy, and especially talking up The Dud, how he was so full of life and how much he looked like Number 2.

Look, I wanted to get the best puppy for our family. If that meant changing our minds and getting Number 1 or Number 3, fine. But I was going to need concrete evidence that something previously unseen in Number 2 had dropped his stock, or that something in Number 1 or Number 3 had propelled one of them to the top of the depth chart.

Of course this "problem" was all about Donna Reece doing

what she's known for doing: producing top-notch Labradors. Not only were the right genetics in place for healthy dogs with breed-standard conformation and calm dispositions, but Donna had done the important work of handling the puppies regularly so they were attached and attuned to humans from the get-go. A rational person might then conclude, "Well, you couldn't go wrong with any of them, right?"

But who said we were rational?

Reason is usually no match for emotion, but that's the course I chose to take with my parents. It went like this:

David: "Okay, you really liked Puppy Number 2 last week and we all agreed he was the obvious choice—smart, calm, curious, cuddly. And he's the same this week, right?"

Dad/Mom: "Yes, yes, he's a wonderful pup."

David: "You still think Number 1 is adorable, but we all concluded last week along with Donna that he might end up being a bigger boy than you want when he's all grown up. Plus, he didn't have quite the gravitas of Number 2, and you liked the buff color of Number 2 rather than all white, correct?"

Dad/Mom: "Yes, but he is a gorgeous puppy."

David: "And I know you say that The Dud has miraculously turned into The Dude, but what if he changes again next week after we bring him home?"

Dad/Mom: "True, but it's amazing how much this dog has changed in a week. You should see these puppies, David. They're all so cute, this is just so hard, we wish you were here. Donna says we can't go wrong with any of them. We just don't know what to do. . . ."

Knowing that my mother likes to make low-risk decisions, I finally played this card, "Mom, the safest choice is Number 2. He is the same pup you saw last week. What you see is what you'll get. You might not end up with exactly what you want with one of the other two."

That was it. The descent started from my parents' emotional precipice. They called me back a couple more times for reassurance and then once more to announce that they were driving home with Pup Number 2 curled up in my mom's lap. Apparently, the deal was sealed when Donna's colleague at the kennel assured my mother, "Mary Jane, you're going to be really happy with this puppy."

Boy, would *that* turn out to be an understatement.

Talk about pressure. I thought the only nerves I would contend with in Cincinnati that week were those that would come during my tennis matches. I didn't realize I would be playing another kind of match over the phone. I felt drained. But I was also exhilarated that a long-awaited dream was riding home in my folks' car. I slept well that night.

Unfortunately, my nearly seventy-year-old parents did not. When we had brought home our previous puppies, we had always followed the practice (a Utilitarian one, I might add) of putting the puppy in a separate room where he or she would cry for a couple nights over being separated from its mother and littermates. This time though, my parents gave in to all the whining coming from the living room and brought the pup into their bedroom, placing him into a cardboard box next to the bed. Minus a few whimpers that were settled by a stroke of the hand, all was quiet on the puppy front the rest of the night.

Puppies generally don't sleep in, so the daily reports from home were about 5:30 a.m. trips out to the front yard with my mother sitting in an Adirondack and the pup sniffing about the acorn-laden lawn before eventually falling asleep under her chair. He was curious and cuddly—just like the puppy I saw in Iowa.

Days passed and I went from the tournament in Cincinnati to the next one in Indianapolis. It was killing me to have to live vicariously through my parents' daily phone calls, "You should see him, he's swimming already, he's so adorable, he's . . ." With intentions of following Richard Wolters' strict training schedule that started on the forty-ninth day, I was wringing my hands and feeling as if the pup would be ruined if I didn't get home soon.

I finally flew home nine days after the pup had arrived (it felt more like nine weeks). When my dad picked me up at the airport, I insisted that he take me directly to his house rather than to mine. He could hardly put the car in park in his driveway before I was out the door and heading around to the front yard.

Like a contestant on *The Price Is Right* with the curtain being pulled back on the greatest prize ever, I could feel myself smiling as I almost ran to the front of the house where I saw my mom and the new puppy sitting on the lawn overlooking the lake.

There was no anticlimax. I may have seen this puppy just two weeks earlier, I may have been part of the drama on take-home day (albeit from afar), and I may have been getting daily reports ever since, but there was something special about actually seeing the puppy for the first time in my parents' yard. He was ours now. The search-and-select phase was over. I was the owner of a Labrador retriever, and he was right there chewing on a twig at my feet. I sat there a long time—a very long time—watching him, holding him, talking to him, taking it all in.

I would be home for only two days before heading out to New York for the U.S. Open. Between tennis practice sessions, I spent nearly every waking minute over at my parents' house with the new puppy. I would have had him stay at my house, but my parents persuaded me that it would be best to keep him in the same sleeping routine for now, "for now" being the operative words.

Over those couple of days, an unending procession of family, friends, and neighbors made the pilgrimage up my parents' driveway to lay their eyes on the irresistible — a new puppy. Almost to a person, the first exclamation out of their mouths was, "Oh, he's adorable!" followed by the question, "What's his name?"

At this point, my mother and I were just starting to play "The Name Game." This is the game that goes round and round for days on end to come up with the perfect name for the puppy. Everyone has a "Here's a great idea!" or a "What do you think of this one?" But most of them hit the ears like an off-key note.

If there are things in life more subjective and with fewer boundaries than naming a dog, I'd like to know what they are. Unlike a child, where, if you're not careful, you can saddle him or her with a burden for a lifetime, you can get away with almost anything for a dog. But we weren't looking for whimsy or trendy — we wanted something where we would look at him and say, "He is *such* a _____."

My mom and I held voting majorities in our name game, but the truth be told, I knew hers held more weight than mine because mothers always hold rank. Compromise could have been possible if there were some common names on both of our lists, but the reality was that we were pretty far apart.

I had a couple rough-and-tumble names in mind, ones that

conjured up images of bravery and adventure. My two leading candidates were *Kodiak* and *Yukon*. You know, names Indiana Jones would approve of. I certainly wanted to avoid anything guys with shotguns would smirk at when we all gathered around the pickup truck. For example, a color-coded name like *Khaki*, or a personality-type name like *Happy*, or heaven forbid, a sugar-coated name like *Snickers*. And I didn't want anything that sounded like *no*. Who wants their dog to think you're scolding him when you're actually calling him? *Beau* and *Joe* were definitely out.

My mom? Well, she was completely unimpressed with my offerings. She wanted a human name (a sure indicator of an Egalitarian) and was settled from the start on just one: *Ben*. This would be short for—get ready to smile . . . or gag—*Benjamin Pooh Bear*.

Ben was a little softer than what I wanted, but hey, it didn't rhyme with *no* and it flowed off the tongue well. And I'll admit, when she said the name Ben, I had one of those outside-the-box moments, where you've been stuck so long thinking in one box, and then along comes someone who introduces something completely different that leaves you contemplating, "Hmmm, never thought of that." I told my mom I would think about it, knowing full well her mind was made up.

Turns out, mother knew best—*Ben* fit him perfectly. His disposition was as soft as his name. He was *such* a Ben.

But there was something my mother didn't know, and neither did I—just how closely my journey with Ben would follow the meaning of his name.

Years later I happened across the biblical account of the birth of Jacob and Rachel's final son.

> When she [Rachel] was in severe labor the midwife said
> to her, "Do not fear, for now you have another son." It
> came about as her soul was departing (for she died), that
> she named him Ben-oni; but his father [Jacob] called
> him Benjamin. (Genesis 35:17–18)

Having a dog by the same name, I was intrigued. Why would
the mother name her son one thing and the father call him something slightly different?

I noticed a footnote next to both *Ben-oni* and *Benjamin*. My
eyes moved to the bottom of the page for the answer. As Rachel
died giving birth, she named her newborn *Ben-oni*, which means
"son of my sorrow." Jacob, perhaps not wanting a perpetual
reminder of this tragedy, called him *Benjamin*, which means "son
of my right hand," denoting a cherished place with his father.

I paused to look down at Ben sleeping next to my desk where
he always slept, under my right side, no less. *Son of my right
hand*, I thought. *That he certainly is*. Everywhere I went, there
he was with me, almost like a son . . . my right-hand man.

But "son of my sorrow"? That certainly hadn't been my
experience. Ben had brought nothing but joy. Life with him was
characterized by hikes and hunts, love and licks, not sadness and
sorrow.

I sat there for a moment contemplating what I had just read.

The next minute I went on with my day, having concluded
that I would side with Jacob on this one.

CHAPTER 5

BOATS, BIRDS AND
PUPPY LESSONS LEARNED

Two days at home went by in a flash, and before I knew it I was boarding a plane from Minneapolis to New York. The good news was that the pup was home and had a name. The bad news was that I would be gone for two weeks.

Of course, going to New York to play in the U.S. Open was not a bad thing, but leaving home made me feel like I would be falling behind in class. Richard Wolters had drilled into my head that "training begins on the forty-ninth day," and I felt Ben would be failing grades if I delayed starting with him any longer.

I soon discovered that I didn't need to worry. In fact, being away for most of that first month had the effect of forcing me out of Wolters' strict week-by-week training timetable and onto a more progress-based training plan for Ben.

What also helped is that my dad and mom were in the process of their own Utilitarian-to-Egalitarian transition. While I was away, they were constantly taking Ben along for the ride where he encountered new people and places, dogs and cars, water and woods—you name it.

They were even unwittingly doing things with Ben that would pay off for me in the pheasant fields later. Tossing a knotted-up sock was just play for my folks and Ben, but it started to ignite his instinctive retrieving desire. And hiding dog treats for him to find in the living room was imprinting upon his mind the most important rule for a hunting dog: use thy nose. I came back from New York two weeks later to a very well-socialized puppy that felt comfortable in his new surroundings.

Comfortable, that is, except in one place: a boat.

Unbeknownst to me while I was out of town, my mom and older brother Mark took Ben out sailing. To my mother's credit, she questioned the wisdom of doing so, but after a "Sure, why not?" from my brother, Ben was taken on board for his first sailboat ride.

The lake was fairly calm in front of my parents' house when they departed, but after sailing away from shore, the conditions turned windy and wavy. If you've ever been in a small, low-sided sailboat in a heavy wind on a big lake with choppy waves, you know that it is a wet and wild experience. With everything soaked and slippery, little Ben slid all over as the boat lurched to and fro in the turbulent conditions.

My mom immediately recognized that Ben was scared out of his wits. My brother, though, the consummate Utilitarian, was far more concerned with keeping the boat aright in challenging conditions than the traumatic effect it was having on a three-month-old puppy. I can just see my mother calling over the wind to my brother, "Mark, he's really scared . . . Let's get back to shore!" and my brother, with his gaze fixed on the sail and hand on the tiller, responding, "He'll be fine!"

Of course Ben never was fine on a boat again, despite my best efforts to gently and gradually reintroduce him. It was a big puppy-lesson learned: anticipate and avoid bad experiences at all costs. First impressions make lasting impressions. In widening his world, do it with great care.

In light of the sailboat debacle, and remembering my friend Sol's golden retriever, Chip, running as if he were fleeing a house on fire after hearing his first shotgun blast, I was very glad to have scheduled an appointment with a professional dog trainer upon returning home from New York. I had heard too many stories of irreversible gun shyness, and so I decided to leave this critical introduction to a pro.

Besides, there would be all kinds of live training birds at the facility that Ben could smell and chase and get excited about. The robins and finches in the backyard of my little suburban plot weren't exactly going to do the trick for a future hunting dog.

Ben was just twelve weeks old when I pulled off the dusty gravel road into Wings and Whistles, a dog training and boarding facility owned and operated by a sturdy man named Mike Schulenberg. The forty-acre property, with Mike's home on one side of the driveway and the indoor and outdoor facilities on the other, exemplified the old adage, "a place for everything; everything in its place."

I can't remember how I had initially heard about Mike, but I immediately liked him when we met. He was not your typical "leave it to me" dog trainer where you drop your dog off (along with your money) and then swallow hard as you drive away wondering what kind of treatment and attention (or lack thereof) your dog is going to get. I could tell that he was a genuine, trustworthy person who was going to do me and Ben right.

Plus, I lived only a short drive away, and since Mike was just going to be introducing Ben to game birds and gun blasts, he was fine with my driving Ben out for the short training sessions rather than having him boarded at the facility.

Mike tackled both objectives at the same time. The old-school way of introducing a dog to the noise of a gun was to take him to the local trap and skeet club and slowly walk him up to the BANGS and BOOMS. This seems like a good way to *discover* if a dog is afraid of gun noise rather than an actual plan to *introduce* him so he won't be. Mike had a much different method.

After we became acquainted, Mike walked across the yard to a large, chicken-wire pen where various training birds were housed, and he returned a minute or two later with a live pigeon in his hand. Whatever Ben had been doing under my feet, it no longer interested him after Mike bent down to gently wave the pigeon in front of Ben's nose. It was as if a switch in Ben's brain was turned to *on* as he inhaled a noseful of bird scent for the first time. Ben didn't know quite what to make of being nose-to-beak with a bird, but it was obvious that he had just connected with his genetic calling.

After about a minute of that, Mike told me to hold Ben in place on the ground as he walked twenty feet away from us with the bird. Heretofore, I thought my new puppy loved me. But now Ben's gaze locked on Mike as if he were some long-lost love. He wriggled with all his might to get away from me and over to Mike and the bird, making me feel as if I had been dumped like a sack of potatoes.

Mike placed the pigeon on the ground. The bird, whose wing feathers were clipped so that it couldn't fly long distances, quickly scampered into some taller grass along the edge of the yard. Lots more wriggling on my end. Ben's anticipation was boiling, and that was exactly Mike's objective.

"All right, let him go," Mike said casually with the tone of having seen this whole scenario play out many times before. As I released Ben, Mike called out in an excited voice, "Hunt 'em up! Hunt 'em up!" Ben didn't need the extra encouragement. He made a beeline over to the bird in about two seconds flat, and a little game of cat-and-mouse . . . er, dog-and-bird ensued.

While the pigeon made valiant attempts to jump and jive away from the clumsy puppy, I could hear the muffled POP of a starter pistol that Mike was repeatedly firing inside a padded sleeve under his armpit. Mike watched Ben carefully to see if he noticed the POPS. Nothing. Not even a lift of his head as if to say, "What was that?" I suspect a jet airplane could have been taking off next door and Ben wouldn't have noticed. Mike was teaching Ben a little subconscious math lesson: chasing birds + popping noises = FUN!

Soon enough, Ben had the pigeon in his mouth, and with his head held high, he proudly carried the fully alive bird back to where Mike and I were standing. Mike took the bird from Ben, gave me an approving look, and said, "This is good—loves birds, no gun noise problems, all bodes well." He ran Ben through the same scenario a few more times and added one more compliment, "He's got a soft mouth." In other words, Ben wasn't chomping down on the bird, but rather, doing what Labs were bred to do— *retrieve* birds rather than crush them.

The whole session lasted about thirty minutes. Over the next couple months, I would bring Ben out to Mike another half-dozen times. It was amazing how Ben would be sleeping quietly in the car on the drive out but suddenly bolt to attention as soon as we turned into Mike's driveway as if to say, "Where's the bird guy?!"

Each successive session kept Ben progressing forward. Wing-clipped pigeons were eventually replaced with fully flying pheasants. The starter pistol fired into a sleeve was later exchanged for a shotgun fired out in the open.

By the final session, Mike had Ben hunting through a narrow strip of shin-high grass, sniffing for birds that Mike had planted.

The strip was so narrow that Ben couldn't help but bump into a bird, at which point he'd flush it into flight followed by Mike setting off a BOOM with his shotgun.

I felt like a father swelling with pride at how my little puppy was getting the hang of this so quickly. Here I had been imagining a far more difficult process fraught with roadblocks and setbacks, but no. There was little Ben searching back and forth in front of us, looking so intent with his puppy tail wagging away. He flushed birds as if he knew exactly what he was doing—just like that dog I had seen on my first day hunting, just like those two black Labs I had seen in the marsh at sunset, just like Gus down at Donna's place.

Ben wasn't at that level yet. Not even close. This, after all, was a controlled environment. Ben had yet to face real hunting conditions with vast fields, wild birds, and the distraction of other dogs, people, and guns, where experience and obedience are essential.

"Just get him on plenty of birds now," were Mike's parting words after our last session. In other words, "Take him hunting." He might as well have said, "Eat ice cream." *Will do! Can't wait!* I was brimming with anticipation.

Ben learned a lot at Wings and Whistles. But I learned something too, something that I had read about in Wolters' book and now had seen firsthand—that socializing and training a puppy wasn't rocket science; rather, it was *proper sequence*. Start simple, progress gradually, and keep it all positive and fun.

The one-block-builds-upon-the-next method I had seen Mike implement was imprinted on me as much as birds and guns were on Ben.

Mike had turned Ben into what hunters call "birdy." Ben's fuse had been lit. Say the magic words—"Hunt 'em up!"—and Ben was off in a flash searching for birds. This level of drive was great, but Ben would also need *control*—in the field, at home, around the neighborhood. "Hunt 'em up" had been learned. "Come on back," among other things, would be next.

CHAPTER 6

TRAINING THE PUPPY ... ER, OWNER

"It's the coach who makes all the difference."

So spoke Sam Mussabini, the idiosyncratic running coach immortalized in the Oscar-winning film *Chariots of Fire*, to his pupil, British sprinter Harold Abrahams.

Mussabini's words may have been slightly on the self-aggrandizing side, but there's no denying that Abrahams went on to win the gold medal in the 1924 Olympic Games in Paris—under the tutelage of Mussabini.

I had seen and experienced enough coaches in my tennis-playing days to know that a coach did, in fact, make a big difference in an athlete's performance—for better or for worse. There were those rare coaches who had the ability to lead their charges to heights that even the athletes did not dream possible. And then there were those coaches who took on athletes with plenty of promise, only to mismanage them to mediocrity.

The latter is what I feared most when it came to training Ben. It was apparent from the beginning that Ben was brimming with innate ability and desire, and as eager as I was to "coach" him to superstardom, I also knew that my lack of dog-training experience could be a liability. I had seen how Mike always seemed to make the right decision. He headed off wrong behaviors before they developed into bad habits and gradually progressed Ben from one step to the next so that Ben was never confused or commanded to do something beyond his capability at the time.

The problem for me was, I didn't know what I didn't know. I had basically read one book on dog training, done a little experimentation on Yogi, and was now in possession of this intelligent puppy with loads of potential who was staring up at me as if to say, "What's next?" Maybe it was paralysis by overanalysis, but I didn't know whether it would be better to say "come" or "here" to call Ben to me. I didn't know whether I should use treats for rewards or not. I didn't know whether I should train him by voice, by whistle, or both.

I did know one thing though, especially after the bad experience on the sailboat; I didn't want to make any mistakes with Ben that would be difficult to undo later. I decided early on that I wouldn't do *some* thing with Ben until I knew it was the *right* thing. Forget Wolters' timetable. Forget visions of Puppy Prodigy. I figured I could still teach Ben things when he was older, but I wasn't so sure I could undo problems that I might cause along the way.

Despite having little background in training dogs, one thing that worked in my favor when it came to training Ben was my background in sports. I wasn't just vaguely aware of what training entailed; I had lived it for almost my entire life. Only this time, I would be the trainer and Ben the trainee. Yet that's not completely true, as every perceptive dog owner comes to realize—training a dog is more about training the owner. You could say that Ben and I both would be trained.

The good news is that I wasn't embarking on training Ben with any feelings of—how shall I say it?—*disinclination* that often accompanied my own tennis training. No matter how much reward I received for my labors, multiple hours a day, year after year spent on the practice court swinging, sweating, and straining dampened the desire for more of the same. Hard work is, well . . . *hard*. And training is always a long and lonely road. The public saw the 1% of my tennis career that I spent on the match court but not the other 99% of toil on the practice court.

When it came to training Ben though, I felt a sense of eager anticipation. Perhaps because it was something new and different, or perhaps because my livelihood didn't depend on it, but working with Ben promised to be a whole lot more fun than work . . . and that's exactly what it turned out to be.

I quickly found out that training a dog requires a lot of thinking both on the micro level when quick, on-the-spot decisions are needed (Is Ben's interest waning and therefore is it time to cut this session short?), and on the macro level in formulating ultimate goals and evaluating whether progress is being made toward them.

Like a father trying to figure out how to raise his son to become the man he wants him to be, I was looking into the future and asking, *To what level of obedience do I need to train Ben? What kind of behavior do I expect him to exhibit around me and others?*

For instance, am I okay with Ben campaigning for scraps by the table, or do I want him to stay in another room during meals? Do I want him to sleep on my bed, or do I want him to sleep in a crate in the porch? Is he welcome up on the couch, or might that be a problem when guests are visiting? How about when we go hunting—is retrieving the bird to within a few feet of me good enough, or do I want him to bring the bird back to me, sit beside me, and hold it in his mouth until I command him to drop it into my hand just as I had seen on the outdoor TV shows?

Ever the contemplator, I found myself giving lots of thought and consideration to these and other living-with-dog questions.

My standards were definitely more strict than what I had seen with permissive-parent Egalitarians who give their dogs tons of slack, apply little discipline, and never say no. The dog basically runs the house. But I was also nowhere in the vicinity of perfect-parent Egalitarians (or for that matter, strict-parent Utilitarians) whose dogs look upward at the owners as they walk on heel, awaiting a twitch-of-an-eyebrow signal to perform the next command. I concluded that the nitpicking required to achieve this level of perfectionism explained why their kids decide to attend college in another country.

Ultimately, what I discovered was that my every interaction with Ben conditioned his obedience and behavior to my personal standards. He simply learned over time what was acceptable and what was not: begging was okay, sleeping in bed was not (well, sometimes); yes, he could come up on the couch, but no, perfect retrieves weren't necessary.

In fact, he picked up my standards quickly because someone (I can't remember who, but I want to thank that person right now) told me that I should "give Ben only the commands that I was willing to enforce." That not only revolutionized the way I gave commands to Ben, but also conditioned him to respond on my *first* command instead of my fourth.

As I mentioned, I used to be the guy who said "come" to his dog (like with Tonka, the Siberian husky) only to watch him ignore the command as if he were deaf. I would say "come" a second time, then a third time, and then a fourth, getting more serious in my tone with each successive command. Meanwhile, Tonka would continue to feign hearing loss while smelling the mailbox in front of the neighbor's driveway three doors down. Flushed with anger at being ignored, I would finally bark out, "TONKA, YOU GET OVER HERE RIGHT NOW OR I'M . . . !!"

Only then would Tonka turn and start to come toward me with no particular sense of urgency as if to say, "Settle down, pal. What's all the fuss?" When he finally arrived, there was no satisfaction of having an obedient dog and no opportunity for a teachable moment. After all, Tonka had just obeyed—even if it was on the fifth call.

The problem was with me, not Tonka. By failing to enforce my command the first time, I had conditioned Tonka not to obey until I repeated the command over and over and eventually raised my voice to threat level. If I had simply said "come" once in a normal tone and then immediately enforced the command by taking him by the collar when he ignored me, Tonka would have learned in short order that "come" actually means he has to come after the first call.

Now I'll be honest; I wasn't perfect about enforcing every command the first time I gave one to Ben. There were my strict-mood days and my laid-back mood days, and of course, the situation at the moment factored in as well. If I was raking leaves in the backyard and Ben was next door, I might give Ben a second "come" before making my way over to him to enforce it. But it was a rare day when I gave him a command three times before a little "remember who's boss" conversation took place. Ben came to learn that a command from me needed to be obeyed, or it would be enforced in short order.

My parents, however, conditioned Ben to a more—how shall I say?—*delayed* response because their "come" and "sit" weren't enforced after the first, second, or even third command. In fact, they never really enforced their commands. They would just say them over and over and then complain to me that "Ben needs to be more obedient." I tried to explain the importance of enforcing commands; but, to slightly alter a dog expression, it was "hard to teach older folks new tricks."

Because my parents and other family members failed to enforce their commands, I was quite certain that my early obedience training with Ben would be all for naught. But that wasn't the case — Ben was far from ruined after spending time with them. He figured out in no time that a command is only as binding as the person giving it.

I'd watch Ben ignore my nephews' commands one moment, but in the very next, he'd do exactly what I told him to do the first time around. This willingness to enforce commands was the difference between an obedient Ben and a Ben that did what he wanted when he wanted. Dare I say it works with kids too?

With the principle "give only a command you're willing to enforce" branded upon my mind, the road was paved for me to teach Ben the three most important obedience commands: "sit," "stay," and "come." Wolters added another to the list that I had never heard of before — a "release" command that Ben could stop doing what I had just told him to do. I used "okay" as my release command; some use "free" or "all right." The word itself doesn't matter, but I found out that having a release command certainly does.

For example, Ben learned "sit" in no time, but his attention span would wane in about five seconds, and he'd get up and wander away. That wasn't going to be good enough, or safe enough. What if I needed him to sit in the driveway for a minute or two while I went into the street to my mailbox? For his own safety, I could not allow him to get up from sitting when he wanted and follow me into the street. This is why a "release" command is as important as the "sit" command. "Sit" means, "Don't move until you hear 'okay' or another command."

It worked great. Ben learned "sit," "stay," "come," and "okay" by the time he was only three months old. From then on, it was just a matter of solidifying these commands and extending the duration of time he could hold them.

Now, having been overtrained myself at times when the last thing I wanted was another day on the tennis court, I purposed that I would make training fun for Ben rather than regimented drudgery. So instead of attempting too many formal training sessions when he was a puppy, I simply took him for a daily walk through the neighborhood and used that time to train him along the way. I slowly built upon what he already knew—a "sit" and "okay" here, and a "stay" and "come" there—always enforcing every command.

I carefully watched Ben's demeanor for the slightest drop in interest. If he didn't chase after the dummy on the fifth toss with his usual gusto, that was the last one I threw for him that day. I found that the old theater adage, "leave them wanting more," applies to dog training as well.

Now, as much as I'd like to say Ben was the perfect pupil and always did exactly what I commanded, that was not the case. There were those times when he would ignore my command to "come" because he wanted to play with the neighbor dog a bit longer, or when hunting, he couldn't resist chasing the pheasants a little farther ahead. Whatever the reason, there were times I had to—perish the thought—punish Ben.

But how? Give him a tongue lashing? Send him to his dog bed without dinner? Make him sit in the corner for a "time out"? How should I scold my baby?!

I had heard various and sundry opinions on how to discipline a dog—everything from "never say a discouraging word" to smacks on the backside. Fortunately, Ben had a soft temperament, so it didn't take much to correct him when he erred from the narrow way. A stern tone was usually enough ("Ben, NO! Bad dog! You *come*!"), but when he was persistently insubordinate, and I sufficiently indignant, I would hightail it over to him, flip him over on his back (which he hated), and give him a face-to-face tongue-lashing and even a shake of the scruff of his neck for extra emphasis.

This little attitude adjustment worked wonders. I could hardly believe Ben's obedience afterward—I could whisper "come" under my breath and he'd be at my side in a flash. "Oh, so your ears *do* work, Ben."

* * *

Ben's training went quickly. I was expecting some multi-year process, but Ben learned everything he needed for my standards of behavior and obedience in the first year. From then on, it was just a matter of reinforcing what he already knew. Sure, I could have continued to teach Ben new things like fetching my slippers, closing the kitchen cabinets, or performing entertaining tricks like standing on his hind legs. I'm sure Ben would have been capable of learning all of this and more.

But all that flash and dash wasn't for me. I just wanted Ben to be able to do what he would need to do in everyday situations at home, on a walk, or out for a hunt. That was enough for me. I used only about a dozen commands with him, although I swear his vocabulary was over a hundred words. And the commands were all basic, like "down," "fetch," "leave it," and "kennel." I didn't see the point in teaching Ben commands that weren't relevant to my life with him. It was far more important to me that he was rock solid on the basics. I just wanted what I think most people want—a well-behaved, obedient dog.

But he went beyond that. If I made a stop on the way home, I could leave my sandwich on a plate between the driver's seat and the passenger seat where Ben was sitting, and when I'd return ten minutes later, the food would be untouched. I never trained him to not eat my food. As a matter of fact, I gave him bites of my food all the time and let him lick my plate after meals, but he somehow knew when it was his and when it was mine.

If I left him outside on the sidewalk while I went into a store, he'd lie down quietly by the front door until I came out. "You mean he'll just wait there for you and you don't need to tie him up?" the clerk or customer would ask, totally amazed. I'd give them the I'm-as-surprised-as-you-are shrug and respond with my usual line, "He just came out of the box that way." Because it's true—he did.

Ben even made me appear to be a better hunter than I actually was. It became a running joke with my family and friends how I would invariably bag more pheasants than anyone else in our hunting group. Why? Because I was some expert shot after a lifetime of hitting moving targets on a tennis court? That was their favored conclusion, but it was more legend than truth.

The real reason was that the dog hunting in front of me found, flushed, and retrieved more birds than the dogs in front of everyone else. This is not to say that the other dogs were subpar (they weren't) or that Ben was "The Best Hunting Dog Ever." It is just to say that I usually ended up with the most birds on a given day simply because Ben gave me the most opportunities to pull the trigger.

There is nature and there is nurture. Ben came with so much

of the former that it didn't take much of the latter on my part. Coach Mussabini said it well, "You can't put in what God left out." My blessing with Ben was that God didn't leave much out.

I don't remember when, but somewhere in the midst of all the training, I discovered that I had one well-behaved, obedient dog on my hands—a gentleman that I could take anywhere.

Ben was all of that, and as you soon shall see, a whole lot more.

CHAPTER 7

SEASONS OF LIFE WITH BEN

How on earth to describe life with Ben? That would be a heap o' life and love to write down.

If page length weren't an issue, I suppose I could compose something of a *Biography of Ben*, chronicling the highlights and everyday occurrences with him. Of course, page length *is* an issue . . . and so is the average reader's attention span. Even the most dyed-in-the-fur Egalitarian readers would struggle to keep their eyelids propped open for too many doggie stories that begin like this:

> You won't believe what happened last week! Ben and I were walking through the neighborhood over to the beach and came across Bunker, that nutty black Lab who blew out a ligament in his rear leg last winter running after the tennis ball; and Ben and Bunker took off toward the front yard, and then . . .

Reality check to self—no one *really* cares to hear every last detail about my "wonderful and amazing" times with Ben. Oh sure, folks are happy to feign interest in a story or two, but unless we are the twenty-first century script for *Lassie* or *Old Yeller*, I'll have to convey all the fun with Ben in simpler and shorter terms.

The early days of puppyhood are easy to remember and fond to recount. I'll never forget visiting Ben's breeder in Iowa, picking him out (or so I thought), seeing him on my parents' front lawn for the first time, showing him around to family and friends, followed by the various and sundry stories of training, housebreaking, and chewing up my slippers, sunglasses, and everything else he could get his little razor teeth on. Years have gone by, but my puppy memories of Ben have never faded . . . and countless pictures and videos make sure they don't.

In contrast, for dog owners, our dogs' final days are something we don't like to revisit, but the sheer weight and pain of the loss won't allow us ever to forget. It is a sad fact that the most recent memories of our dogs will also be our last. I wish it weren't so, but as night follows day, losing a dog *always* follows loving one. We all know this and we try to avoid thinking too much about it, but it rarely stops us from getting a dog in the first place. We assure ourselves that it is "better to have loved and lost than never to have loved at all." And this is true.

So while the beginning and the end of our dogs' lives have their unique peak-and-valley stories, it's what takes place in between that is important to convey. And it's not so much about the high-lights—like the time Ben gulped down the entire ice cream cone from the hand of my nephew or made the incredible retrieve all the way across the lake. These are funny and amazing, but they hardly tell of the myriad of days and ways Ben was just "there" all those years.

It's the little stories with Ben that make up the one Big Story. And where I live, it's a story influenced by the seasons.

Winter, spring, summer, and fall in the Upper Midwest are remarkably distinct from one another. So distinct that six months on the calendar means a one-hundred-degree change in temperature. Each season, in its own unique way, affects everything, from the clothes we wear and the activities we pursue to the social interaction we have with our neighbors . . . and our dogs.

And that is why a glimpse into my seasons of life with Ben is the best way to frame the diverse portrait of our life and times together.

* * *

Just after "The Great Minnesota Get-Together" (otherwise known as the state fair), the early signs of autumn are subtly, yet unmistakably felt and seen, with the breeze turning a bit more brisk and the occasional maple tree showing a tinge of color. With warmth behind and cooler days ahead, you might think the mood of folks in the northland would follow the inexorably descending temperatures. Not so. For many, even most, and definitely for Ben and me, fall is the most beautiful and enjoyable season of the year.

In September and October, as the leaves went about making their transformation from green to various hues of red, yellow, and gold, I took Ben on several trips up north to our family cabin. If you ever hear Minnesotans refer to "up north," as in, "We're heading up north this weekend," they are referring to the northern two-thirds of the state, which is mostly forested and dotted with thousands of lakes.

I, like many Minnesotans, go up north to spend time at the cabin, which—now that I think of it—probably needs further translation too. "The cabin" is a catchall term that Minnesotans use to describe a broad spectrum of dwellings, from rudimentary, summer-use only, small wood shacks with no running water, to large, four-season, multimillion-dollar homes with the latest and greatest creature comforts. Whatever the style, "the cabin" usually sits on or near a lake.

Our cabin in the far northeastern corner of Minnesota is located on what is known as the "North Shore." This is a stretch of coastline along Lake Superior where my parents had taken their honeymoon half a century earlier, and which became a favorite vacation destination for our family. We love the wild beauty of the area; the big views of "the big lake" (Superior is the largest body of freshwater in the world); the hiking and skiing; rugged landscapes; wildlife sightings of moose, wolves, and bald eagles; and canoe trips into the wilderness region known as the Boundary Waters Canoe Area (BWCA).

A longtime dream became reality when we bought our cabin on the North Shore. The routine of heading up north each autumn had already been established before getting Ben, but little did I know that adding Ben would bring so much greater enjoyment to a place we already loved. In fact, once we had Ben, going up north without him was unthinkable. That would be like leaving the most important necessity of the trip back home!

Ben figured out early on when we were heading up to the cabin and made sure he wasn't going to be left behind (he didn't need to worry). I'd be packing my bag and the car, and all of a sudden he'd go missing. I'd always find him in the same place—already having jumped into one of the open doors of the car, fast asleep for the long ride north.

No doubt one of the reasons that Ben loved going to the cabin was the opportunity to explore remote forest trails in search of a game bird that is native to the state—the ruffed grouse. About the size of a chicken and considered the best-tasting of all game birds, ruffed grouse, named for the "ruff" of black feathers around their necks, were a favorite quarry of Ben's and mine.

Whereas pheasant hunting is often done in groups of four or more with multiple dogs in the expansive grasses and sloughs of open farm country, grouse hunting is typically a solitary pursuit with one person and one dog wandering down a quiet forest trail.

I had never experienced anything like this kind of man-and-his-dog picture-book grouse hunting in the years before getting Ben. Like others without dogs, grouse hunting for me had consisted of slowly driving the gravel roads of the north woods, hoping to spot a grouse, at which point I would quickly stop the car, get my shotgun out, and try to fire a shot before the grouse flew off into the woods. This method was mostly fruitless and not much fun.

But now with Ben, my old army-style Jeep that was kept at the cabin would serve solely as a means of transport over the ridgeline that rises above Lake Superior. And then we'd drive farther back into the woods until we arrived at an old logging road or narrow trail where we would get out and walk. "Drive around and find 'em" would no longer be my mode of operation.

Our walks in the woods always started the same humorous way. With shotgun in hand and Ben hovering around my feet in full-alert mode, I'd look down and teasingly ask him, "Are you ready? Are you sure you're ready? Do you want to find a bird?" This was like pouring gasoline on the fire that was already burning inside of him. YES! He was ready. And YES! He did want to find a bird . . . more than anything else in the world at that particular moment. As if preparing to launch, he would stand there steady and stiff with his eyes locked on mine, waiting for me to utter the magic words. "Hunt 'em up!" I'd finally say, and in a flash he'd turn and tear down the trail.

I had lots of time with Ben on these walks, and that was the best part. Time to wander through colorful falling leaves on a sun-striped trail. Time to tune in to the forest and observe tracks of deer and moose. Time to sit on a fallen log and share a snack. Time to walk down to the creek and watch Ben wade in for a drink. Time to appreciate the athletic and artistic movements of a beautiful hunting dog doing exactly what he had been bred and loved to do.

Ben was top notch at grouse hunting, too, what with his highly attuned nose and insatiable desire to keep searching here, there, and everywhere for a grouse. I have no idea how he navigated through the tangled woods so adeptly. He'd jump over that log, slip under those evergreens, and weave his way through dense thickets all the while checking for scent along every inch of the forest floor on both sides of the trail.

My job was to keep close watch on his tail. Once it started to stiffen and swing, I'd better be ready because a grouse, invisibly camouflaged on the forest floor, would soon be rocketing up and careening away through the trees.

Even with Ben's tail-alert system, grouse were still difficult to bag. The bird is renowned for its uncanny ability to flush quickly and escape through the woods, never giving the hunter a clear shot. I didn't so much care that another one got away, but I always felt as if I had let Ben down. He had done his part. Why couldn't I have done mine?

Another element of the North Shore experience that was so enriched by Ben's presence was our annual fall canoe trip into the Boundary Waters. As the name implies, the Boundary Waters is an extensive wilderness area of lakes and woods in northeastern Minnesota that extends a hundred and fifty miles along the international border with Canada. Being a federally protected wilderness, there are no roads, no cars, no motorboats,

and very few human beings anywhere within the BWCA. Your
only travel option is to park your car where the road ends and
enter the wilderness with a canoe and paddles.

It's quite a place, the Boundary Waters, with enough wilderness
and wildlife to make your average suburban boy squirm when he
realizes Starbucks (and help) is not right around the corner, and
that the few items in his backpack—tent, sleeping bag, clothes,
food—will be all there is for the duration of the trip.

In the years just prior to getting Ben, my brother Mark and I
had traveled each fall into the Boundary Waters for a few days of
paddling, camping, and exploring. Ben stayed back at the cabin
with my folks for his first couple years, but then one September,
when I was sure that he had made the transition from puppy to
dog, I decided to take him along. Mild objection was raised by
my brother, "He'll tip over the canoe. He'll get lost. He'll attract
wolves." But I persisted, and there stood Ben one day with my
brother and me on the shore of an uninhabited lake with our packs
and canoe ready to enter the wilderness. Never again would we
take a trip into the Boundary Waters without Ben.

Now that I think of it, the idea of taking a dog on a wilderness
canoe trip is a perfect litmus line between Utilitarian and Egalitarian. There is really no practical reason to take a dog on this
kind of adventure, and that would be the end of the discussion
for most Utilitarians. Ben couldn't provide protection from bears
or wolves. He couldn't help carry gear on the trails between
lakes (called "portages"). He wouldn't be hunting grouse for
us to eat. The truth is, having him along was pretty much pure
liability. Staying warm and dry is of utmost importance, and the
inclusion of a dog in a tippy canoe decreases the likelihood of
that. Plus, if Ben were to get injured, or cause one of us to get
injured by tripping over him while carrying a canoe or a heavy

pack over the rocky and slippery trails, it could mean a day or two of paddling just to get back to the car to seek medical help.

As I said, there is no good reason to take a dog on a wilderness canoe trip. But we Egalitarians don't think like that. All I could imagine was the enjoyment of having my boy along for the adventure. I pictured Ben sitting between my legs in the canoe as we paddled across the lake, having him snuggle up around the campfire at night, and sleeping between my brother and me in the tent. It all seemed perfectly logical to me. And fun. Yes, it sounded really fun having Ben along.

And it was. Ben absolutely loved these autumn trips and yes, my brother loved having him along too. The experience and the memories just wouldn't have been the same without Ben.

* * *

I like to remind friends from warmer parts of the country, who just can't believe that I live in Minnesota because of the frigid winters, that one of the great things about the state is that Bing Crosby's famous song is pretty much unnecessary here. One doesn't need to *dream* of a white Christmas because the overwhelming odds are that there will be plenty of the white stuff already on the ground by then.

In fact, once Thanksgiving arrives, give or take a week, you can pretty much count on the lakes freezing up and snow coming down until early April.

Having lived on a lake for most of my growing-up years, I vividly remember watching and waiting for "The Day." That is, when the open water on the bay in front of our house froze into a mirror-like sheet of ice. This was the first phase of the winter playground in front of the house, where I would spend the season skating, cross-country skiing, and dog sledding.

And those were just the things I liked to do. Others came out on the lake for the ice fishing, ice boating (think of a sailboat with skate blades), or any number of other activities such as snowmobiling, snowshoeing, or being towed behind a car on a sled. Yes, people drive cars on the frozen lake once the ice is thick enough—another "can't believe" for my southern friends. In fact, that's how I exercised Ben when I was feeling too lazy or too cold in the winter—by having him chase behind my car on the lake.

The skating portion of the season is generally short-lived because the next snowfall is never too far away, thus blanketing the ice and ruining the bliss of being able to glide over the smooth surface for miles on end. Time is of the essence—some years you get two weeks to skate on the lake, some years two days, some years no days at all. This short window of time for skating is so prized that my mother would let me stay home from school for a day or two to enjoy it when I was a child. Thank you, Mom.

So when Ben came to be, he was destined to be my skating companion. It took some coaxing to get him out on the newly frozen ice for the first time. There he was, sitting in the yard, trying to figure out how on earth I was standing on top of the water that he had been swimming in a few weeks earlier. My sweet talk prevailed, however, and he eventually took his first steps, gingerly and nervously, onto the mirror-like sheet of ice, looking like he wasn't so sure about all this. You can understand the trepidation. Standing on an inch of ice and looking straight down to the bottom of the lake, wondering if and when you're going to break through into the freezing water can be slightly disconcerting.

Ben overcame his reservations in fairly short order though,

and came to enjoy running next to me as I went for long skating treks across the lake. For him, there were new places to smell and new dogs to meet as we passed by the vast stretches of shoreline.

Ben didn't rue the day, as I did, when the snow came down and made skating impossible. That's because he loved cross-country skiing even more. On ice, he didn't have the advantage of skate blades that could propel him forward with minimal effort to keep pace with me. Even with four legs and toenails—starting up, slowing down, and changing directions were tricky propositions.

But with snow came traction for him. Cross-country skiing, at least the traditional kind I do, is slower than ice skating but faster than walking—perhaps about the same speed as jogging. I dare say Ben liked skiing more than hunting, but it was close. All I had to do was gather my skis and poles from the garage and he'd become all atwitter. It was pure freedom for him—no leash, open spaces, cool weather, a good run.

Before I had Ben, winter never kept me from getting outside, but when he came into my life, I was out in the snow and cold almost every day. That's one of the great things about having a dog like Ben. It forces us to get outside and be active. With the signature heartiness of a Lab, Ben didn't even seem to notice the cold and loved getting out on a frozen lake or a backwoods trail. And I loved nothing more than being there with him.

* * *

Sometime in late March, when the sun begins to linger longer and higher in the sky, just at the point when those folks who cherish winter (yes, cherish winter) have enjoyed another season of skiing, skating, and snowmobiling; of wearing sheepskin-lined slippers and woolen sweaters; of sipping warm soup by the fire on cold, dark nights; of snuggling under the down comforter for a long winter's nap; spring emerges and offers a whole new season to experience. From April into May, everything changes—frozen lakes melt into open water, leafless trees explode with new life, birdsongs fill the air again, flowers pop up and bloom out of nowhere, and people appear as if coming out of hibernation.

In Minnesota, spring inspires a "Wow, it's balmy out there!" feeling when the thermometer rises *all the way* to 50 degrees for the first time since, well, five months ago in November of last year.

At the first sight of open water in spring, Ben was in it. The edges of the lakes melt first, and Ben would be wading in as if the water temperature were 80 degrees rather than 40. The mere sight sent a chill up my spine, but he didn't give it a second thought.

In spring, Ben and I would get back on the roads for our daily exercise after a winter of going out on the frozen lake. As nice as it was to feel the warmer air, see the budding trees, and talk to neighbors again, there was a downside; the snow that had covered the ground all winter slowly disappeared to expose sandy streets and soggy lawns. This transition on the ground resulted in another transition—on Ben's coat, from shiny to filthy.

I pretty much felt like a dog-cleaning service in spring. Let Ben out. Clean Ben off. Let Ben in. Repeat. The only sanity saver is that Labs have a kind of self-cleaning coat. If you leave them outside long enough, things tend to improve (at least that's the hope). Now that I think of it, that's probably why Ben spent a whole lot more time outside in spring—a nod to my Utilitarian roots, no doubt.

* * *

If the cold and dirty seasons in the northland—winter and spring—are why folks head south, then summer is what brings 'em back. Who wouldn't want to soak in those long summer days with highs in the mid-70s, perfect for any and everything, where the sun and cotton-ball clouds spend their time jostling for position in the sky? There will be some swelter to endure now and again during July and August, but that is the exception rather than the rule.

It is said that there are nine months of winter in Minnesota and three months of tough sledding. An exaggeration this, but its power of suggestion is not—Minnesotans do feel an urgency to get it all in while summer's in session because three months is all you get. Most everything in summer revolves around the "sky-tinted waters" (as the Dakota Indians aptly named the Land of Ten Thousand Lakes)—whether cruising, sailing, or paddling about on some sort of craft, and fishing, tanning, or tubing while doing so. Even folks who aren't out on the lake will likely be found jogging, biking, camping, or dining next to one.

Summer is the most popular time of year for Minnesotans to go up north to the cabin. Not so much for Ben and me. We stayed around home most of the time for one specific reason—tennis practice.

While tennis is an individual sport, one can't do it individually. In other words, you need a sparring partner on the other side of the net. And unless I arranged for a practice partner to trek up to the cabin with me, there wasn't going to be a whole lot of tennis prep going on there.

So during the weeks I was home during the busy summer tournament schedule, Ben and I would make the daily thirty-minute drive across town to a tennis club where I would sharpen my skills with a local teaching pro.

Mind you, dogs aren't generally welcome at private clubs,

especially when a non-member like me brings one. But it would have been difficult for anyone to complain because it would have been difficult to even know that Ben was there. Once the car was parked, he'd jump out of the passenger seat (of course), follow me to the side of the court, and then lie down quietly as I went through my paces for the next couple hours.

All he asked was that I hit a few tennis balls for him to retrieve after the practice session, which I always gladly did.

The members who did see Ben were charmed by him and asked the usual question, "Is he always that well-behaved?" What could I say? He was born with his head screwed on straight. For all I knew, Ben spent the time beside the court deep in thought about the finer points of the game after having watched me play it for so many years. In fact, he would have been a good ball boy if I had ever figured out a way for him to deliver the balls to me without their being so unplayably soggy.

At this late stage of my tennis career, having Ben along for the ride, the practice, and the sprints at the football field afterward, made the daily training regimen not just bearable, but enjoyable.

We'd often stop by my parents' house on the way home to take a swim with my mother. Her father had passed down his love for swimming to her, and she continued the tradition by taking a daily, late-afternoon swim around the perimeter of the bay in front of her home. It was a half-mile and usually took three-quarters of an hour—much more than a quick dip. After a day spent sweating, it was a good way to cool down.

Taking the family dogs on this distance swim was nothing new. Back in the days of our Siberian huskies, my mother would literally drag them off the dock (tied together, Utilitarian style) to accompany her around the bay. They complied (there wasn't much choice), but I got the distinct sense that they weren't thrilled at being in the water for that long.

Ben had no such reservations. One might think a dog would get tired swimming all that way, or have trouble keeping up, what with our wearing flippers and hand paddles. But the reality was that our swimming aids were our only chance of keeping up with Ben! He would zip out front, look back to check on the slowpokes, and then circle around waiting for us to catch up.

Ben was an unusually proficient swimmer, even for a Lab. I had seen some Labs flailing away when they swam, head up, legs splashing about, and looking half-panicked. Not Ben. From his first days in the water, he had a low-profile swimming technique that propelled him forward like a torpedo.

Tennis, swimming, cookouts, walks by the lake, Memorial Day and Independence Day celebrations. These are all ordinary summer activities where I come from . . . yet all made extraordinarily better with Ben.

* * *

If you think this is a rose-colored look at life in the northland, you're right—I failed to mention the mosquitoes. But my point in describing my seasons of life with Ben has nothing to do with making the case that Minnesota is the best place to live or to convince you to come on up for a vacation. You may live in a very different place, perhaps among the skyscrapers of Manhattan or near the beaches of San Diego. You could just as well write your own description of the climate and culture where you call home and why your heart is forever enmeshed with the seasons of life in your area. The old proverb is absolutely true: home is where the heart is.

And that is precisely my point: to give you a little taste of where my home and my heart are so that you have a deeper sense of how Ben's constant presence by my side during each season year after year added something so special to my life that I would have never experienced had he not been there.

This led me to ponder a simple question—why did I love Ben so much? The answer may seem obvious, but I still felt compelled to truly understand.

CHAPTER 8

FOR THE LOVE OF DOG

Imagine for a moment that the day has finally arrived for you and your family to appear as contestants on your favorite television game show of all time, *Family Feud*. You still can't figure out how your wacky family made it through the selection process (hey, maybe wacky *was* the reason). But there's no time for that now. You've been flown out to Hollywood and are about to walk onto the set in front of hundreds of screaming fans in the live audience, with millions more watching on national television.

Remember—deep breaths.

You and the other four members of your family take your places stage right, while your opponents do the same stage left. With the theme music blaring and everyone clapping and cheering, the studio announcer crescendos his introductions by welcoming "the host of *Family Feud*, Richard Dawson!"

Dawson, the original and iconic host of the show, emerges from behind the curtain in one of his signature 1970s-styled suits looking sharp but acting slightly tipsy as if he had just downed a swig or two of the hard stuff before coming onstage.

On a tight clock, but acting as if he's got all the time in the world, Dawson eases into pre-game formalities by asking you to introduce each member of your family. You proceed to do so as Dawson, with his trademark British accent and dry wit, adds bits of humor and fluff. Both families duly recognized, Dawson makes his move toward the center-stage podium shouting out, "Let's play the Feud!"

The mood in the theater turns quiet and focused as you and your opponent go to the podium to face-off for the first question. Standing between the two of you with question card in hand is Dawson, who quickly gets to the point. "One hundred people were surveyed; the top six answers are on the board. You have to try and find the most popular answers. Here's the question: why do people love their dogs so much?"

Wham! In a flash, you and your opponent pound your respective buttons, with you getting there a millisecond sooner. You have the faster hand, but now, do you have the better answer? You blurt out the first thing that comes to mind, "Unconditional love!" As if in unison, all eyes on stage and in the audience converge on the huge board that backdrops the set, where the six correct answers are hidden from view. To your complete elation, a DING breaks the tension as the first of the six hidden answers flips over, confirming that "unconditional love" was, in fact, the most popular answer in the survey.

You're stunned—not so much because you got the top answer, but because this was, unbelievably, the question that was asked when it was your family's turn on the Feud! You are among the biggest dog lovers in the history of dog lovers! There has never been a time in your life when you haven't had a dog. You treat your dogs better than the kids ("because they're more obedient," you like to joke). You all watch Westminster every year as if it's some religious experience.

You look over to your family for what you already know is

going to be a foregone conclusion. Having won the face-off, you can either choose to play and have your family try to come up with all the other answers, or you can pass the question over to your opponents and hope they "strike out" by making three wrong answers, which will then provide you the chance to "steal" the round by giving just one of the remaining answers left on the board.

No surprise here—your family believes with their every fiber that they can come up with the other five answers. You tell Dawson, "We'll play!"

Dawson saunters over to your side of the stage, where the members of your family are practically bubbling over with anticipation. Dawson first approaches your wife, who is next in line, leaning over to give her a kiss, as is his custom with every female contestant. She has already heard the question but he re-reads it anyway: "Why do people love their dogs so much?"

Your wife confidently states something she's told you a million times about your dogs, "Because they are such great companions!"

Dawson turns around, looks up at the survey answer board, and yells, "Companionship!" DING turns the second answer on the board.

Dawson moves next to your married daughter, who says sweetly, "I love my dog because she always gets me in a great mood!" DING goes the board to reveal that the third most-popular answer is "Improves happiness." "Great mood," "Improves happiness" . . . same difference for this show.

Feeling the wind at your back with only three answers remaining and zero strikes against your family, your son-in-law, who didn't grow up with dogs but now "gets it" because he's been around your family, casually states, "People love their dogs because they're entertaining." A little murmur of doubt rises from the audience, but sure enough, number four on the board turns . . . DING. *I knew there was something I liked about that kid*, you think to yourself.

Dawson then makes his way to the end of the line, where your teenage daughter has been patiently standing. Having had to wait for everyone else to go before her, and worrying that her answer would be taken, your sixteen-year-old bursts out, "Because dogs are fun to be with!" *Too general, too vague, too obvious*, you think. Before you can even put a period on the thought, DING sounds from the board, and over flips answer number five.

Surprised, elated, and suddenly feeling as if the table is about to be run, the turn comes back to you at the front of the line, where you can now seal the deal. But the problem is, what could the sixth-and-final answer be? You thought you could have given a hundred answers to this question, but now you can't seem to come up with one more reason people love their dogs so much. You certainly don't want to be the first member of the family to get the big BUZZ for a wrong answer, but not giving an answer will bring about the same result. Sensing your distress but needing to follow the rules, Dawson quietly tells you that you have five seconds.

Suddenly, out of nowhere, an answer pops into your head. But you're afraid to say it. You know it will cause embarrassment, especially if it's wrong. Figuring your kids are almost grown, your boss isn't watching, and your wife will understand (oh, please!), you say reluctantly, "Well, Richard, uh, I don't know if I should say this, but, uh, men, uh, love dogs because they work great for . . . meeting women!"

The audience erupts into gales of laughter as your wife blushes and contemplates which side of your face to slap. You try to subtly remind her that this is how you met her on the jogging trail way back when, but this has no effect on simmering her boil. It's obvious, however, that Dawson is liking the direction the show has just taken. He turns, points to the board, and yells with glee, "Meeting women!"

As if on cue, the last unrevealed answer flips over for the final DING, launching your family and the crowd into rapturous applause and celebration. Your family wins the round and takes a big lead. And you? You're out of the doghouse.

Now, truth be told, I had never watched *Family Feud* enough to know whether "Why do people love their dogs so much?" was ever an actual question in a real game. But if it were, I'm pretty sure the survey would say that these six and a few others like them would be the most popular answers. It's true, a good dog is—and does—all these things.

I found myself often pondering the same question about Ben. Why did I love him so much? It seems like such an elementary question, even unnecessary, one where the answer is so patently obvious that the minimal mental exertion required to contemplate it is hardly worth the effort.

But the question just kept coming up with Ben. I'd be nearing home in my car and all of a sudden would feel a surge of anticipation come over me as I pulled into the driveway looking forward to seeing Ben. I never felt anything close to that with our other dogs. And why is it that any event in my life, even the mundane ones—a walk, an errand, a meal, a nap—was that much more enjoyable with Ben by my side? What was it about this particular dog, Ben, that brought such a palpable joy to me?

I didn't approach the question as some academic exercise where data would be collected, analyzed, and then presented on PBS to explain the historical and sociological connection between canines and Homo sapiens. No, it was far from that, something much more basic. I just wanted to know what was behind this deep love I had for Ben. Was it something about him, or was it something about me, some new phase of life I had entered, or perhaps a void inside of me that needed filling?

I was quite certain that I hadn't suddenly morphed into a Universal Dog Lover (UDL). You know the type. They basically melt over every dog they encounter. Even if it's a complete stranger's dog that they met two minutes earlier, the UDL will be down on the ground in a flash, playing and pampering and baby-talking away, slobbering on about how much they love dogs . . . *all* dogs.

I loved dogs in *general*, but I never was a UDL and didn't become one after having Ben. Sure, I always give attention and a few pets to someone else's dog, but I have never felt the inner compulsion to be an equal opportunity Universal Dog Lover. In fact, I'm not ashamed to admit that I love my own dogs exponentially more than other people's dogs. That doesn't seem too abnormal. Those we love the most are typically those we know the best and those with whom we spend the most time. I'd let Ben lick me on the face any day. But another dog? I have my standards.

Having concluded that I wasn't a UDL, I began to surmise that there must be something unique about Ben that caused me to love him so deeply. After all, I enjoyed our previous dogs — Muffy, the sweet half-Lab, half-Samoyed; and Tonka and Tinka, the troublemaking but endearing Siberian huskies. But I never thought about them as much, never felt the need to have them with me all the time, never missed them as much when I was away, never dreaded losing them as I did Ben. It's not like I didn't love them, because I did. It's that the *depth* of my love for Ben went to a completely different level.

As I've mentioned, Ben had this nobility about him, a soulful, serious temperament, and an intelligence and ability to learn and perform, which at least partially explains why I loved him so much. He exceeded his breed's reputation for being good-natured, eager to please, and easy to train.

He was a "backdoor dog." When I'd let him outside, he'd sniff around the yard for a few minutes and then return to fall asleep by the backdoor, patiently waiting to come in to be by my side again. There was no bolting, no disappearing acts, no need for invisible fences—he was just trustworthy and faithful. What's not to love about a dog like that?

I know, these are personality- and performance-based reasons for loving a dog. You could say it's a variation of the Golden Rule for dog owners—we love dogs who do well unto us. It's always easier to love the angel-child more than the inveterate rebel. Ben was the angel-dog. As my mother liked to say, "Ben never did anything wrong." It's true—he always seemed to do the right thing to keep himself out of trouble and on the straight and narrow.

So there was something special about Ben that caused me to love him so much. But I also wondered what it was about me that predisposed me to love him the way I did. In fact, I went so far as to question whether something might be off-kilter with me or my human friendships such that I needed a dog to fill the void. You know, the whole "single guy's best friend is his dog," or worse yet, "thirty-something is afraid of marriage so he finds love in man's best friend."

My closeness with Ben no doubt led some friends to these kinds of conclusions. They'd receive my annual Christmas card with yet another "Ben-and-me" photo on the front or watch me drive by with Ben riding shotgun in my Jeep, and the single-man-and-his-dog narrative would be solidified.

I certainly won't deny the companionship angle—Ben *was* a great companion to me. And he was a great companion at an especially fitting time in my life. When I got Ben, I was nearing thirty, living alone, becoming very interested in pheasant hunting, and spending more time at home toward the end of my pro tennis career. What could be a more ripe scenario for a man getting a dog?

But that shouldn't be translated as meaning I was some lonely, socially inept guy who didn't have a life or family and friends and therefore needed a dog to fill that void. To the contrary, I had plenty of friends and a close family who lived nearby. And even when I did stop competing full-time on the tennis tour in my early thirties, I was busy transitioning into a new career in radio broadcasting while still keeping my tennis game up for the smattering of events I would play in the summer, such as World Team Tennis and the "seniors" at Wimbledon and the U.S. Open. My life was full and fulfilling.

And as far as needing Ben because I was "commitment averse" with women, let me just say that I spent my thirties not running away from women, but wrestling with two fundamental questions about marriage. Was I actually the marrying type? And if so, who was the right one to marry?

For whatever reason, I had never assumed that I would get married someday. Like most red-blooded males, I did have interest in girls in my teens, twenties, and thirties, and was involved in some serious relationships along the way, but I never came to the point of concluding that "this is the one for me, for life." That's how I had been raised to think about marriage—as a lifetime commitment—and my parents had modeled this to me and my siblings in their fifty-plus years of marriage. I knew marriage was a very big deal, and I wasn't going to be jumping in until the desire and the damsel were right.

The leading candidate for most of my life had been a girl named Brodie. We grew up as family friends, having known each other since our single-digit days when I was eight and she was five. Being four grades apart in school didn't help the cause, however (High school seniors don't often notice the eighth graders, right?), and it wasn't until I was in my early thirties that I was able to get beyond the brother-sister dynamic and actually date Brodie for the first time.

What everyone thought was meant to be didn't turn out to be. After one year, right at the end of my full-time tennis touring days when it would have been logical to take the next step, we amicably broke up . . . and continued to remain friends.

I was shaken but still not stirred about marriage, which of course feeds the "What's wrong with you?" look from others when you're well into your thirties and unmarried. I didn't see it that way. My operating mindset was that I would strive to be "contentedly single until shown otherwise." After witnessing too many divorces and less-than-stellar marriages, I knew it was far better to be single, even unhappily single, than to be unhappily married. And I was far from being unhappily single.

Meanwhile, throughout my season of singleness, Ben was there by my side being the great companion he always was. Contrary to what some people thought, I never felt in the least that my closeness with Ben somehow diminished my desire to date or kept me from getting married. Far from it. As a matter of fact, I had visions of Ben carrying the ring box down the aisle at my wedding!

So what was my conclusion as to why I loved Ben so much? Was it because he was such a great dog? That was certainly part of it. Or did I love him so much because I had him during a unique stage in my life? That was certainly part of it too.

Both of these reasons point to something even more foundational—I loved Ben so much because he *enhanced* my life so much. Having Ben made everything I did in life better, sweeter, more enjoyable, more interesting. All the top answers in the *Family Feud* scenario—unconditional love, companionship, happiness, entertainment, fun, and meeting people—what do they imply? They all say in slightly different ways that having a dog adds something extra, something wonderful to life that wouldn't be experienced without a dog.

It goes without saying that a dog greatly enhances the life of a disabled person, a policeman, a shepherd, a soldier searching for hidden explosives in a war zone. These folks and many others who have dogs for reasons beyond canine companionship couldn't do what they do without dogs. *Enhance* maybe isn't the right word; for each of them, a dog is a necessity.

For a regular dog owner like me, however, all I had to do was consider how much Ben enhanced even the simple things I did in life. How much more enjoyable was a walk with Ben than when I strolled alone? How much better was it to come home to Ben rather than an empty house? How much nicer was it to have Ben snuggled up next to me as I read or watched TV than to be the only one in the room?

Ben made the fun things more fun and the mundane things more interesting. Work became more enjoyable with the bits of humor and distraction he brought each day. Even life's disappointments were softened just by having my best boy there with me.

Dogs enhance our lives. Great dogs enhance them even more. That's exactly what Ben did for me, and that's a big reason why I loved him so much.

But there is another fundamental reason why I loved Ben. It

goes down to one of the deepest and most basic human needs and desires, and that is *relationship*. I had come to understand this in a more spiritual way in my early twenties when I became a Christian and read in the Bible that God designed men and women not to be lone rangers, but rather to be in relationship with other living beings—with God, with humans, even with animals.

Some of the opening sentences of the Bible show God's relational intent.

> Then God said, "Let Us make man in Our image, according to Our likeness; and let them rule over the fish of the sea and over the birds of the sky and over the cattle and over all the earth, and over every creeping thing that creeps on the earth." God created man in His own image, in the image of God He created him; male and female He created them. God blessed them; and God said to them, "Be fruitful and multiply, and fill the earth, and subdue it; and rule over the fish of the sea and over the birds of the sky and over every living thing that moves on the earth." (Genesis 1:26–28)

This passage is full of relationship. God created two humans, a male and a female, to be in a "horizontal" relationship with each other and in a "vertical" relationship with Him. God also created the animals and placed them in a vertical relationship under humans. Everything here speaks of relationship—differing types and capacities, yes, but relationship nonetheless.

I found it interesting that God, in and of Himself, is the model for relationship. God refers to Himself in the plural, "Let *Us* make man in *Our* image according to *Our* likeness." This refers to God's triune nature—that He is one unified being with three distinct persons: Father, Son, and Spirit. I won't attempt to explain that, but the takeaway point is that God has relationship amongst Himself, and He made humans in His image to be relational as well.

It made sense that when I was in a right relationship with God and had good relationships with other people, I would be living according to the purpose for which God created me and would experience a heightened sense of fulfillment and meaning. It also explained the opposite—why I felt unhappy when I neglected my relationship with God and when I was at odds with other people.

But what about my close companionship with Ben? I often wondered, even struggled with, whether my relationship with him could and should be as meaningful as with God and others.

I thought and searched and mulled over what the Bible says about man's relationship with animals. From the passage in Genesis, I knew that we are to be good stewards of animals. I had also read in Proverbs that "a righteous man has regard for the life of his animal," which was a clear statement that we are to treat animals with dignity and respect.

And then I came across a well-known story in the Old Testament that showed the kind of relationship a man could have with an animal, and it forever put to rest any doubts about whether I loved Ben too much.

Almost everyone has heard about King David's adulterous affair with a woman named Bathsheba, which resulted in a child, and David's arranging for the murder of Bathsheba's husband. This was the lowlight of David's otherwise illustrious life, and he nearly lost everything over it.

When I read how Nathan, the prophet at that time in Israel, had confronted David about his great sins, I was struck by the analogy he used to drive home his point.

> The Lord sent Nathan to David. And he came to him and said, "There were two men in one city, the one rich and the other poor. The rich man had a great many flocks and herds. But the poor man had nothing except one little ewe lamb which he bought and nourished; and it grew up together with him and his children. It would eat of his bread and drink of his cup and lie in his bosom, and was like a daughter to him. Now a traveler came to the rich man, and he was unwilling to take from his own flock or his own herd, to prepare for the wayfarer who had come to him; rather he took the poor man's ewe lamb and prepared it for the man who had come to him."
>
> Then David's anger burned greatly against the man, and he said to Nathan, "As the Lord lives, surely the man who has done this deserves to die. He must make restitution for the lamb fourfold, because he did this thing and had no compassion."
>
> Nathan then said to David, "You are the man!" (2 Samuel 12:1–7)

Nathan's point was abundantly clear. David was "the man," the rich man with the large flocks who had stolen the one beloved lamb (Bathsheba) from the poor man (Bathsheba's husband). It was unjust, unconscionable. David needed to repent (and he did).

But it was the story itself that Nathan used to convey just how deplorable David's actions were that resonated so deeply within me.

There were countless other scenarios Nathan could have used to get his point across: man with ten kids takes away another man's only child; rich man steals another man's last penny.

But instead, Nathan describes in touching detail the tender relationship between a poor man and his one little lamb, and how all of a sudden, a heartless rich man enters the peaceful scene and shatters it. The egregiousness of the offense is highlighted to the maximum through a storyline that would arouse repulsion and condemnation in any feeling person.

It certainly did with King David. After hearing Nathan's parable, David didn't respond by saying, "What's the big deal? It's just an animal. Give the poor man a couple new lambs to cheer him up and let's get on with life." He didn't say, "What's wrong with this guy, treating his lamb like a daughter?"

Instead, David went to the other extreme—a place where only the most devoted pet lover would go. David was so moved by the close relationship the poor man had with his lamb and so enraged at the injustice of the rich man's actions that he was all set to execute the rich man. "As the Lord lives," he said, "surely the man who has done this deserves to die."

When I read carefully over the words again and saw how much the poor man loved his "one little lamb," how he "nourished" it and how it "grew up together with him and his children," how it would "eat of his bread and drink of his cup and lie in his bosom," and how it "was like a daughter to him," I realized that this kind of relationship between man and animal was not odd or unnatural, but actually beautiful and good. It was Ben and me. Ben ate from my plate and lay in my lap. He was like a son to me.

After reading this, I knew that if it were wrong for a man to have such a close relationship with his pet, then God wouldn't have inspired Nathan to use the story. And David wouldn't have been convicted by the point of the story if the man's relationship with his lamb was so strange or wrong.

This helped me realize I didn't need to feel unsure or ashamed of my relationship with Ben. This Bible passage implicitly affirms it is a precious thing to love one of God's creatures like a member of the family.

Now, before taking the relationship between man and dog to ends unintended, let me say that, as much as I loved Ben, I knew I couldn't and shouldn't expect my relationship with him to replace or hinder my relationships with God and other people.

God made me in *His* image, and not in the image of animals. Therefore my capacity for relational depth and meaning is always going to be far greater with God and men and women because of our likeness to each other. I have the ability to relate to and communicate with another person on an intellectual, spiritual, and social level that Ben could not match.

It's interesting to note that God, after creating the animals and the first man, Adam, said, "It is not good for the man to be alone" (Genesis 2:18). In other words, animals were able to provide *some* relationship for Adam, but apparently it wasn't good enough. So God created the first woman, Eve, to be a companion in his same likeness.

I draw this distinction not to wax theological, but rather to remind myself that having a close connection with God and people will always be more important and fulfilling than my relationship with Ben, even considering how close and meaningful he was to me.

This may be "Well, duh" for some (Utilitarians are nodding), but for others (Egalitarians), this is not what we always want to affirm. We've been hurt too badly by people and sometimes we think God is too distant and unknowable. Meanwhile, here comes my boy Ben wagging his tail and licking me on the face, and . . . well, what more is there to life than that?

There is no question that Ben was almost always *easier* to love than a person. Whoever said, "It's no coincidence that man's best friend can't talk," was on to something. Unlike people, Ben never wounded me with words. Rather, he communicated unadulterated affection.

But there are real words of conversation, of counsel, of consoling, of correction that I need to hear, and Ben couldn't provide that. The mutual-admiration relationship I had with Ben certainly made me feel good, but like anyone else, I needed some "truth spoken to power" at times. In a sense, Ben's love was *too* unconditional—it overlooked things about me that could have used some refining.

What I really needed to do was follow the relationship priorities God established in the "Greatest Commandment."

> "You shall love the Lord your God with all your heart, and with all your soul, and with all your mind. This is the great and foremost commandment." The second is like it, "You shall love your neighbor as yourself." (Matthew 22:37–39)

Love God most, then others. No mention of animals here, but that is what makes the wonderful relationship I had with Ben all the more amazing. Ben and I weren't even of the same "kind," and yet it's as if God wanted me to experience even more relationship, feel even more love by designing me with the ability to relate so well to Ben. I could love Ben and still love God and others even *more*.

I finally found the answer to my question. Why did I love Ben so much? Because he enhanced everything I did in life and because he satisfied, in part, God's relational design for me.

And it only magnified over time. Puppy Ben took quick hold on my heart, but after laying down a few years together, the degree of life enhancement and relationship ascended to amazing heights. His dependence on me only further cemented our bond because I knew he needed me for care, for nurture, for affection.

Unlike the kids, he wasn't moving out, and neither was I. It was the two of us together, through the seasons of life, all the way to the end.

CHAPTER 9

A GENTLE NUDGE

The lake had frozen particularly smooth that December, and knowing there might be only a day or two to enjoy it before the snow came, I made the easy decision to drop everything and get out for a skate with Ben.

It was a rare afternoon on the lake, and as far as I could tell, Ben and I were the only ones out to savor the majestic scene. Like a black mirror, the ice perfectly reflected a darker shade of the blue sky and brown leafless trees along the shoreline. Daylight was in short supply this time of year, and by mid-afternoon the sun was already low and arcing toward the western horizon.

Ben was where he always was when we went skating—about ten yards behind me and in a fast trot. Every other activity we did together—walking, swimming, hunting, cross-country skiing—he was out in front, but with ice skating, two blades were faster than four paws.

We soon found ourselves skating along an especially affluent stretch of shoreline where the "old money" lived on the lake. These were the multimillion-dollar estates with large homes on sprawling, beautifully landscaped grounds that had been originally purchased by the founders and presidents of the big-name corporations in town and now were occupied by their progeny a generation or two hence. *Money can't buy happiness*, I reminded myself as I glided by, *but it can certainly purchase some nice real estate.*

I did a quick one-eighty so that I could skate backwards to watch Ben. He had that happy-dog look on his face—ears flopping, mouth open, and tongue dangling off to one side. This was way more of an outing than our usual walk through the neighborhood, and he was loving it. His gait looked like that of a wolf crossing the open tundra—not a galloping run, which would have been warranted to keep up on any other surface, but rather a fast, keep-as-many-paws-on-the-ice-as-possible trot that minimized slippage, while still moving ahead with speed.

He was a vision of grace and beauty, a healthy eighty-two pounds of muscled athleticism, and more prized to me than any expensive home we were passing. If any one of the homeowners had offered to trade their luxurious property for my dog, I would have turned it down in a second. "I'll give you a million dollars for your Lab," I imagined one of them saying.

"Forget it," would have been my immediate response. Ben was priceless to me.

While continuing to skate backwards, I pulled out my phone and snapped a picture of Ben running toward me. The photo recorded the stark scene—in a vast, inanimate background of ice and sky, there was Ben, one blond spot full of life and luster, the very picture of health. If you had told me that this would be my last winter with him, I wouldn't have believed you.

It's not that I had never thought about life after Ben. In fact, that sobering reality came up every so often in conversations with my mother. We both realized early on just how special this dog was and just how much he enriched our lives. He had an inestimably high value to us, and so it was only natural to perish the thought of losing what we treasured so greatly.

We were realistic enough to know that he wasn't forever though, and thus we had these melancholy exchanges from time to time. One of us might be relaying to the other something Ben had done or some sweet aspect of his personality and then the thought would be spoken about "how hard it's going to be to lose him someday," and "how we need to appreciate him while we can."

It wasn't something we obsessed over. But it was there, as it is for every dog owner. And yet it seemed so many years away and more theoretical than anything else. All our previous dogs had lived long lives into their early teens, and Ben was only eight. I figured I had at least four years left to enjoy him, maybe six. Besides, I took great care of him, fed him quality food, got him plenty of exercise, and took him to the vet at the slightest sneeze. If any dog was a candidate for longevity, it had to be Ben.

I skated on toward the neighborhood where my parents, sister, and brothers and their families all lived. Christmas was right around the corner and I felt blessed. Everyone in my family was in good health, and we would soon be getting together to celebrate the holiday as we always did—Christmas Eve service at church, turkey dinner with all the fixings at Dad and Mom's, reading aloud Luke's account of Christ's birth, exchanging a few gifts, and singing some carols while the logs turned to ash in the fireplace. Ben would be there as usual in the middle of it all, sporting a red ribbon around his neck that had been recycled from an opened present.

After thirteen years of traveling all over the world on the tennis tour, I was enjoying being home for times like this. My new career as a radio host was fulfilling, and I even sensed that my lifelong friendship with Brodie might be headed toward something more permanent. We had been seeing more of each other the previous four months, and this time seemed more natural, more serious, more headed for engagement than the first time we had dated some five years earlier. Life was good, very good, and Ben and I on the front of my Christmas card for yet another year illustrated that.

Typically by this time of year I had already made the transition from fall activities, like hunting and hiking, to winter pursuits, such as ice hockey and cross-country skiing. Even though the pheasant season was technically open for a few more days into early January, my shotgun was usually cleaned and hanging on the wall by this time, as I had learned from experience that late-season pheasant hunting in knee-deep snow was more about trudging than walking for both man and dog.

But this year, as December was about to become January, there had been less snow than usual, and with sunny and mild temperatures in the forecast and a few remaining days of vacation, my brother John and I decided to head out for one final junket into pheasant country accompanied by his twelve-year-old son Johnny.

On New Year's Day, the three of us and Ben left early from Minneapolis and drove three hours west to the border of South Dakota, where I knew a couple farmers who were always nice enough to allow me to hunt on their land. This was an exciting outing for my nephew. He had passed his hunter-safety training course and only recently had been hunting for real with us, rather than being a tag-along observer as he had been in previous years. It was an equally special time for his dad and uncle to have him officially be "one of the hunters" and perhaps see him bring home a lifelong memory—his first pheasant.

Ben made sure soon enough that there wouldn't be a "perhaps." He was such a proficient hunting dog at this point that hardly a word needed to be spoken from me to him. After seasons of experience, he was at his peak, with his intelligence, obedience, athleticism, and great nose all fully developed and working like a well-oiled machine. Think of the "wow" you get when you watch world-class athletes do their thing—that was what Ben was giving me every time we went out hunting.

Within ten minutes of entering the field, Ben stopped abruptly thirty yards in front of me and froze with his head up and ears perked, looking intently into a clump of grass in front of him. I could tell right away from his body language that he was "pointing" a hiding pheasant.

This was Ben's standard operating procedure when a pheasant opted to hide in place rather than run ahead. Even though he was a Lab and therefore technically a flushing breed, Ben pulled off a pretty good imitation of a setter or a pointer on this score. I never trained him to do this; he just did it instinctively . . . and it was highly advantageous to be hunting with this advance-alert system.

A pheasant won't stay put forever though, so I quickly hustled up to Ben while calling to my nephew to hurry over. This would be the perfect set-ball-on-tee opportunity for Johnny to get his first pheasant after going home empty-handed (and a little disappointed) in previous outings. It seemed like minutes before his twelve-year-old legs could get him through the prairie grass and over to Ben and me. Thinking that the pheasant would take off or Ben would rush in at any moment, I kept urging, "Hurry up, Johnny!" But Ben didn't move, and neither did the pheasant.

Finally, Johnny arrived, and I started stuttering out a dozen tips and instructions all at once. "Get your gun ready! Don't forget to take the safety off! Be sure to aim in front of the bird! Don't shoot too quickly! Make sure Ben is out of the way!"

Poor kid—here I was, cluttering up his mind when there were only two things that really mattered: whether this hiding pheasant was in fact a male and thus legal game, and if so, whether Johnny could safely connect with a shot.

Meanwhile, Ben and the unseen pheasant were still in the middle of their little standoff. After waiting a few more seconds, I realized that I would have to intervene to break the stalemate. So with Johnny now standing next to me and holding his gun in full ready position as if he were about to call, "Pull!" at the local skeet range, I looked down at Ben and said, "Get 'em up, boy!" With his look-before-you-leap personality (which is the reason I think he didn't rush in on holding pheasants in the first place), Ben repositioned himself a couple times around the clump of grass before eventually moving in nose first. To no one's surprise, a pheasant, and a big, colorful rooster at that, exploded upward in a loud burst of wings from the thick tuft of grass. How this colorful bird had been able to hide right in front of us was beyond me.

The bird had flushed so close to us that I immediately concluded that this was sure to be Johnny's first pheasant, taken over a picture-perfect point by Ben, no less. All Johnny had to do was raise his gun, track the bird as it flew away, pull the trigger at about twenty-five yards, and there's his lifelong memory. Johnny had proved himself a capable shot with clay targets, and so this rather large, close-range pheasant shouldn't be much of a problem, right?

Wrong. Johnny did the first two steps just fine . . . and then didn't pull the trigger. I watched as the pheasant quickly put distance between itself and us, first at a nice and close twenty yards, then a little farther at thirty yards but still well within range, then quickly to forty yards (*Uh, Johnny, you might want to pull the trigger now*), and finally to the point of being nearly out of shotgun range at fifty yards away.

Well, I guess that one's gone, I thought. *Why didn't he shoot? Did he forget to take the gun's safety off? Is he having second thoughts about shooting a pheasant? How am I going to console him after missing this perfect, close-range opportunity?* All those questions were summarily vaporized with a loud BOOM! With one shot—a very long shot—Johnny had done it. I watched the pheasant fall like a rock, instantly dead in the grass fifty yards in front of us.

I couldn't believe it. I couldn't believe Johnny had waited so long to shoot. I couldn't believe that he had dropped a pheasant from that far away. And I couldn't believe my nephew had just bagged his first pheasant right in front of me over a point by Ben. And there was Ben, carrying the bird back to us in his mouth. I started stammering, "Great shot, Johnny! . . . I can't believe it! . . . Why did you let it get out so far? . . . Are you excited? . . . Hold the pheasant next to Ben for a picture!"

Okay, so I was a proud uncle.

We went on hunting the rest of the day, and then drove a couple more hours west and checked into a hotel in Huron, South Dakota, where we were to hunt the next two days with some good friends who lived in the area. We stayed in adjoining rooms—father and son in one room, and Ben and I in the other. I turned out the lights around 11:00 p.m. with me sleeping in the hotel bed and Ben in his dog bed on the floor. I occasionally let him sleep on my bed at home; but for hotels, I brought his dog bed, figuring that subsequent guests might not appreciate my Egalitarianism.

I was in a deep sleep in the dark room when I was awakened by a soft nudge on my arm. It was Ben's nose. I groggily looked at the clock on the bed stand, trying to figure out where I was and what time it was. The red digital numbers on the clock read somewhere in the vicinity of 1:30 a.m.

Ben usually slept through the night. In fact, he was a late riser, always waiting for me to get up around 8:00 a.m. Very rarely did he wake me up during the night to let me know he needed to go outside to "do his stuff." If he did need to go, he never whimpered or whined—it was always just a gentle nudge.

I wearily got up. With the outdoor temperature barely above zero, I wrapped a jacket around my flannel pajamas, pulled a knit hat over my head, and stuck my bare feet into untied boots to make the short trip downstairs to let Ben outside.

Ben knew all about staying in hotels, so I didn't need a leash to walk him down the hallway and into the elevator to get to the lobby. Once there, I let him out the back entrance. He immediately hustled over to get underneath the branches of an evergreen tree. I watched him from about fifteen yards away, my head poking out the door and feeling the frigid night air. Sure enough, he had diarrhea. *Poor thing had to go*, I thought. *No wonder he woke me up.*

Ben getting up in the middle of the night with diarrhea was uncommon, but not without precedent. If you have a dog, you know how they eat stuff they shouldn't, and voilà, they get a bout of diarrhea for a day or so. Or sometimes during prolonged exercise like hunting, Ben's stools would become softer, so I figured the previous day's hunt may have had something to do with it.

Whatever the reason, I wasn't too concerned as we retraced our steps up to the room and climbed back into our respective beds. I was back asleep in about two minutes.

I was awakened by another nudge around 4:00 a.m. and this

time I knew what it was about. When you have diarrhea, it usually entails more than one trip to the bathroom. So I wasn't much more concerned this time as we made our way to and from the lobby for another trip outside. Still, two trips out during the night was definitely not the norm, so I decided I would feed Ben several small portions of food the next day rather than his usual one meal in the morning and one meal at night in an effort to not "overfeed" whatever was going on inside him.

Aside from a touch more diarrhea upon exiting the hotel in the morning, Ben was acting his normal self as we loaded gear into the back of my SUV. He ate his breakfast with complete gusto and seemed no worse for what had happened during the night.

It was a beautiful day to be outside. The weather was sunny with temps expected to reach 40 degrees — downright balmy for early January. Ben hunted as beautifully as the day in these perfect conditions, flushing or pointing all kinds of pheasants, retrieving downed birds, and generally being the pro he had become.

As nice an outing as it was, however, I didn't like the fact that Ben made several stops throughout the day for more short bouts of diarrhea. He'd stop, relieve himself, and be back hunting in a flash. Suspecting that this must be depleting his system, I made sure to give him plenty of water and small amounts of food as the day wore on.

Over dinner that evening, I discussed with my brother whether I should hunt Ben the next day, which would be the last day of our trip. Ben's disposition and energy were normal but obviously something inside of him was not. I went to bed deciding to do what I did when I was battling an illness or injury in the middle of a tennis tournament — see how I felt in the morning and make a game-day decision.

The night went the same as the previous, with Ben waking me

up a few times to go outside. I was tired in the morning, mostly from interrupted sleep, but also from trying to figure out what was going on with him and what I should do. It had been only a little over twenty-four hours since his first bout, but I didn't like this. I was so tuned in to Ben that any slight change in his behavior set me on notice right away.

The difficulty with Ben was that he didn't show much when he wasn't feeling well. I had to learn the hard way when he was younger not to let him overwork himself while hunting. He would go and go and go to the point that he'd become wobbly on his legs. I had never had a hunting dog before and assumed when a dog became tired or overheated that he or she would naturally slow down. Not Ben. He had an insatiable desire to find the next bird and wouldn't stop until I stepped in.

That is what I should have done on this day. But I was torn. I didn't want to shut down the trip early for my brother and nephew. I also didn't want to disappoint Ben. He was not a whiner, but the one situation in which he would cry like a baby was when I left him in the car to rest while we walked off with shotguns in hand. Even with the windows closed, I would hear him yipping and yapping as if he were being subjected to cruel and unusual punishment.

To leave Ben inside the vehicle to watch us for the *full day*? I couldn't bear to do that to him. So with plenty of hesitation, I made the decision to let him hunt.

It was a day I will never forget. Ben hunted as if he were possessed. To borrow a tennis expression that is used when someone is playing far above their regular level, Ben was hunting "out of his mind." Even my brother, who hunted frequently with Ben, couldn't believe him. It was like Ben had shifted into overdrive, quartering back and forth with the utmost urgency, sniffing here, there, and everywhere to find the next pheasant. The dog was on a mission.

In the afternoon, we worked our way around the edge of a large marsh where Ben pointed pheasant after pheasant. Most were hens and therefore off limits, but we didn't mind — this was like having a front-row seat at a professional hunting dog clinic. He was flushing or pointing so many birds that I eventually put my gun away and pulled out my camera, following behind him and snapping pictures as he zeroed in on one after another.

As great a day as it was, I was glad when it came to an end. I didn't like that Ben had been stopping again for diarrhea in the midst of hunting so hard. I was hoping he would have eased off the intensity, hunted a little more casually. But he had done the opposite. He'd hunted like a fiend, as if he knew it was the last day he'd ever hunt and he wanted to go out at the top of his game. But I had a strong sense he needed to stop, and the end of the day — the end of the entire season for that matter — made sure that would be the case.

We walked out of the marsh and up a long hill to where the vehicles were parked. Ben was walking by himself behind us with a pheasant in his mouth. Moments earlier, he had found, flushed, and retrieved this one final rooster, and I could tell he wanted to carry it all the way back to the truck instead of handing it over to me. I let him. He deserved a little extra reward after how hard he had worked.

I watched Ben coming up the hill. He was as focused as ever. He took his hunting seriously all right, as if it were his calling. In fact, he pretty much took everything seriously. Far from a goof-off, he went about his life doing exactly what he was supposed to do and doing it very well. But now he looked tired carrying that pheasant back to the vehicles. I'm guessing he knew this was the final day of the trip and that we would be making the long drive home soon. I don't know how he knew these things, but he did.

We crested the hill and took in a panoramic view of the western sky. It looked like a painting by God. The glowing sun was sitting like a huge fireball on the horizon and setting half the sky ablaze. The wispy clouds above were colored various pastel shades. Behind us to the east, the direction we would soon be heading, dusk and darkness were taking over.

I didn't know it at the time, but it was a moment of foreshadowing. Daylight was setting on Ben and me. A dark time was moving in.

We said our thank-yous and good-byes to our friends and drove out of the field onto a two-lane paved road. It would be five hours of this in the dark the whole way home. Nothing much to see, but plenty of time to think. We hadn't put a mile behind us before Ben was already fast asleep in his crate. He hardly stirred. I kept hoping to hear him sit up or change positions or just do anything to let me know he was feeling okay. But nothing.

We stopped halfway for food and fuel, and I was barely able to coax him out of his kennel. By the time we arrived home a couple hours later, I had to lift him out. He just stood there on the driveway looking dazed. It was the middle of the night on January 3, and the wonderful trip we had just experienced was the farthest thing from my mind. I'd seen Ben tired after these trips, but this was different. I was worried about my boy.

CHAPTER 10

ULTRA UNEXPECTED

Ben seemed to be feeling a little better in the morning, though it was obvious that he was still tired. This was pretty typical for him for a day or two after a hunting trip; even the most well-conditioned athletes need time to recover after intense exercise.

His energy level was not my main concern though. It was still the diarrhea. That is why I called the vet clinic first thing to see if Dr. West, Ben's regular vet, had any openings. He didn't. Not wanting to wait another day, I took the first available appointment with one of the other doctors and was soon driving over to the clinic with Ben.

When the vet came into the exam room, I related to her all that had happened over the previous two days. After a thorough hands-on examination, she didn't find anything obviously wrong with Ben but said that we should know more after testing Ben's stool sample that I had collected that morning.

It turned out that wasn't conclusive either. But the vet did have a hunch. She thought it likely that Ben had a case of giardia, a fairly common parasite that gets into the small intestine of dogs (or people) through eating or drinking contaminated food or water, causing all manner of gastrointestinal problems. I was well aware of giardia from our canoe trips into the Boundary Waters, having been warned to boil water from the lake before drinking it. This we did.

The diagnosis made sense to me. On any given hunting trip, Ben was in and out of the many streams and waterways that run through the agricultural fields. I figured that he had lapped up some giardia-tainted water on the first day of the trip when I wasn't looking, which would explain his diarrhea.

The good news is that giardia doesn't have serious long-term effects—two to four weeks until the bug gets out of the system—and it can be treated with medication that reduces the symptoms and longevity. So out the clinic door I went with a couple weeks' dosage of medication and some easy-on-the-stomach canned dog food, relieved that Ben's troubles would soon be under control.

But not much changed. For the first few days after the vet visit, Ben's stools improved a little, which was encouraging, but they were still far from normal. I figured it might just take some time to rid his system of giardia or perhaps the canned dog food wasn't agreeing with him. Whatever it was, why was he still waking me up two or three times each night to be let outside?

These wake-up calls were starting to take a toll on me. This was the closest thing that I had ever experienced to caring for a newborn, and I quickly developed a new appreciation for mothers having to answer a baby's irresistible cry during the night. Ben may have been a gentleman about letting me know he needed to go outside; but still, after one week of this, I was exhausted. Not just physically exhausted from being awakened multiple times a night, but mentally exhausted from trying to figure out what was wrong, and emotionally exhausted from worrying about him.

Feeling like my wheels were spinning and I was running out

of steam, I wrote Dr. West an email to ask about other treatment options. Ben had been on the medication for six days, and I expected some improvement by now. I was ready to do what I had been taught from my tennis-playing days—"change a losing game." Dr. West thought otherwise, however, responding that giardia can be difficult to diagnose and treat, and that finding the right medication is the key. Thus we should stick with the path we were on for the time being.

One more week passed. It was mid-January in Minnesota and winter had finally arrived in force—snow, cold, and all. Ben finished his course of medication and canned dog food, but nothing had changed. Except for one thing—his appetite.

This was not a turn I was expecting. Ben had always been a voracious eater. Put the food in his dish, and it was gone in less than thirty seconds. He was like one of those dogs in the dog food commercials that rushes over to the dish and gulps it down as if he hasn't eaten in a week. After having dogs that were finicky eaters in the past (my mom would add gravy and scraps and heat up the Siberian huskies' food—oh brother), we couldn't get over how Ben would chow down the same dry kibble every day with such gusto. Ben not eating well? Big red flag.

Another week went by and a second stool test was done. The results were inconclusive again. The decision was made to try a different medication. One more week passed. Still the same soft and odd-shaped stools. Still waking me up at night. Still lacking appetite.

Another week, a third test. This time no giardia found. Good news, right? Then why did Ben still have diarrhea? Why was he losing his appetite?

What on earth is going on with my dog?

The questions were piling up and the answers weren't coming.

I felt as if I were in a pitch-black room trying to feel around for a light switch that didn't exist. January came to an end, and nothing was making any sense.

* * *

Super Bowl Sunday arrived on February 4, and some family and friends gathered at my parents' house to have dinner and watch the game. Even for non-hardcore football fans like my family, the Super Bowl is a good reason to get together for an American tradition. There were about fifteen people in the living room that night. Everyone was paying attention to the game . . . except my mother. She couldn't take her eyes off Ben, who was lying on the floor next to my chair. "Ben can't get comfortable," she kept saying to me with a concerned look in her eye.

It was true. Ben was changing positions every few minutes as though his stomach was sore. His demeanor was down as well. The contrast in the room couldn't have been more stark: festive occasion, dispirited dog.

I had scheduled an appointment the following day with another vet in our area to get a second opinion. Nothing against Dr. West and his clinic—they had done all the appropriate tests and treatments. I just wanted to see if all of us were stuck in the same box with none of us thinking outside of it.

The doctor we visited for a second opinion was the same vet we had seen for our Siberian huskies way back when. My parents and I crowded into his exam room, at which point I detailed Ben's history over the past month. He examined Ben and performed some of the same tests as Dr. West had, including a stool test for giardia, which came back negative again. But he did do one thing that had not yet been done—he ordered a series of abdominal X-rays.

A surge of anxiety went through my mother and me when the doctor explained why he wanted to take X-rays. He ticked off the possibility of seeing a broken rib or a foreign object. That seemed serious enough . . . until he mentioned a third possibility—finding some kind of mass. The very thought that we might be dealing with something far more serious than a case of chronic diarrhea—like cancer, for instance—was almost paralyzing.

To our great relief, the abdominal X-rays showed nothing abnormal. We left the office with more medication, more canned food . . . and a prophetic report from the doctor: "Ben's giardia and direct smear tests were negative for giardia. We took abdominal X-rays today, which do not reveal any obvious tumors, masses or foreign bodies. If the diarrhea continues, then I recommend referral for an abdominal ultrasound or colonoscopy."

A "referral for an abdominal ultrasound" would take place just three days later. In the short time after the appointment, Ben began to exhibit increasingly unusual behavior. During a walk with my mom, he stopped to lie in the snow on several occasions as if trying to cool off his stomach. He also seemed to be having some trouble urinating.

My mother couldn't take it anymore. On Thursday, February 8, she called our regular vet. He wasn't available, but another vet at the clinic was—Dr. Lisa Logan. Dr. Logan had been a vet for more than twenty years but was unknown to us because she worked part-time at the clinic. It turned out that Dr. Logan's specialty was internal medicine, precisely what Ben's problem called for. This "chance" phone conversation between my mother and Dr. Logan turned out to be a divine appointment, for she would figure most prominently in Ben's care from that day forward.

After an extended conversation with my mother and a review

of Ben's case, Dr. Logan decided it was high time to schedule an abdominal ultrasound at a vet hospital in town that performed specialized diagnostic tests for pets. Dr. Logan didn't want to wait a week or even a day for the ultrasound—we would be heading over for the test that evening.

I sat with Ben in the backseat of my parents' car as we drove to the vet hospital for the ultrasound. It was dark outside, and Ben was lying calmly next to me. This was not his usual calm, though—he seemed to be an uncomfortable calm. My boy wasn't well and hadn't been so for quite a while now. My mom, always one to jump to the worst-case scenario, brought up her greatest fear, "I just hope this isn't cancer." My dad, the level-headed, just-the-facts type, responded by giving a few logical reasons why it most likely wasn't.

I wanted to agree with my dad, but we were treading in a world of unknowns at this point. We hoped the ultrasound would shed some light on what had been taking place with Ben for more than a month now. On the other hand, we were fully aware that new news could be bad news. "I just can't believe that Ben would have cancer," I said out loud, trying to reassure myself. "It must be something more straightforward."

The conjecturing concluded as we turned into the parking lot of the clinic. We entered the lobby, checked in, and sat down. It wasn't long before a serious-looking woman came into the lobby through a door that led to the back half of the building, apparently where the diagnostic testing took place. She introduced herself as the doctor who would be doing Ben's ultrasound and then got right to the point about what the test entailed.

Whereas X-rays are preferred for viewing hard internal structures like bones and joints, she said an ultrasound is more effective for viewing soft tissues and organs such as the stomach, intestines, bladder, and kidneys. Normally when people think of an ultrasound, they envision a doctor moving a hand-held wand over the "baby bump" of a pregnant woman to check on the condition of the child inside her womb. Apparently this doctor would be doing much the same thing with Ben; only she needed to shave some of the fur off Ben's stomach first so she could capture better images. I didn't want Ben to be shaved, but it seemed like a small inconvenience if it meant finding out what was wrong with him.

The doctor's explanation was over as quickly as it started, and I suddenly realized that the moment had arrived for her to lead Ben out of the lobby. I had imagined that we would go into an exam room, where the vet would give Ben a once-over, answer all our questions, and then take him to the back for the test. But apparently the lobby was going to serve as the consultation room and this was going all too quickly. An uncomfortable feeling came over me, as it always did, whenever I watched Ben being led away behind closed doors at the vet. I didn't like anything being done to Ben without me by his side.

We quickly offered up a few questions, trying to stall the proceedings. "What do you think this could be?" came from my mother, hoping that the doctor would respond with a likely but harmless diagnosis.

The doctor wasn't about to play the guessing game. "We'll know more after the ultrasound," she deflected.

My father followed up by asking, "What kinds of things will you be looking for?"

This was a good question, a technical question, and the doctor replied by ticking off a range of possibilities from fairly benign to "more serious." We all understood what "more serious" meant — cancer. The C-word. It pained us to contemplate this, but we had to face up to the possibility.

I pretty much knew the answer to the next question, but I asked it anyway, "If Ben does have cancer, will you be able to see it on the ultrasound?"

The doctor had probably performed hundreds if not thousands of ultrasounds on dogs, and I was quite sure she could easily spot obvious cases of cancer. What I was really asking was whether I could be receiving unbearable news within the next half hour. Waiting a week to find out the results of the ultrasound would be hard enough, but finding out in a matter of minutes, when an ultrasound hadn't even been on our radar this morning? I wasn't ready for this.

The doctor answered my question in the ambiguous way doctors often do, not wanting to commit herself one way or another. I knew she had to do that just in case the ultrasound images were inconclusive and other tests were needed. But I could read between the lines — she would most likely be able to tell if Ben had cancer.

There wasn't anything else to say or do at this point besides turn Ben's leash over to her. She walked him across the lobby toward the same door from which she had first appeared. Ben went slowly, looking tired.

My parents and I sat quietly for a few moments, staring into blankness, thinking, hoping, worrying.

And then my dad suggested we pray.

Prayer wasn't out of the ordinary for our family. My parents were committed Christians and had been for longer than my thirty-seven years of life. They talked the talk, and more importantly, walked the walk. Faith wasn't something they just did on Sundays. The Bible was held up as the Word of God and their guidebook for marriage, raising kids, and living life. So for my dad, praying wasn't like rubbing a rabbit's foot or keeping fingers crossed or hoping for good luck. The Bible said that prayer was our way of talking to God and pouring out our hearts to him. And so my dad did just that.

We leaned into each other and bowed our heads right there in the lobby chairs. My dad earnestly prayed that the doctor would be able to gain a clear understanding of Ben's problem, and that if it was God's will, Ben would be found to have nothing seriously wrong with him. He also prayed that we would receive strength and calm. "In Jesus' name, Amen," he concluded. And then we sat quietly, waiting for the doctor to return.

She walked Ben back through the lobby door sooner than I anticipated. Less than thirty minutes had passed. I looked into her eyes as she came toward us, trying desperately to discern good news or bad news. I couldn't read her. She had the same neutral expression as when she first introduced herself.

As before, she got right to the point: "The ultrasound showed that Ben's prostate is about five times the normal size." Before we could ask what that meant or what would cause that, she continued, "Ben either has a highly inflamed prostate or prostate cancer."

"Which do you think it is?" I immediately responded.

"I think it's likely that Ben has prostate cancer," she replied soberly with a touch of empathy in her voice and on her face.

I looked in her eyes and knew that she was right. Horrible, awful, gut-wrenching right.

She went on to say that she had performed a physical check of Ben's prostate gland and found it enlarged. She also extracted some cells that would be sent out for testing. Tomorrow we would get the final answer from the lab as to whether Ben did, in fact, have cancer.

None of us broke down or cried. We were too stunned to have the worst-case scenario all of a sudden be the scenario. Ben, now lying by my side again, looked the same as he had a half-hour earlier, minus the shaved stomach. But *everything* had changed since he had walked back through that door.

The doctor told us that only two types of mammals get prostate cancer—male humans and male dogs—and that the disease is much more prevalent in humans than dogs. And to make things even more confounding, a neutered dog, like Ben, was highly unlikely to get it. Here we were hoping and praying that Ben had something simple and treatable; instead, we were quickly gathering that we had the "rare case" on our hands.

As the conversation continued, I began to sift through my limited knowledge for anything I knew or had heard about prostate cancer. Thoughts like "one of the more common cancers" and "treatable and curable if discovered early" and "pretty good life expectancy" all went through my head. In other words, even in the face of this difficult diagnosis, I had some hope that Ben's prostate cancer would be treatable, maybe even curable, and that he would be with us a lot longer.

All those thought bubbles of hope were burst a moment later when I asked the doctor about the prognosis for Ben. For the first time, she used a qualifier before giving her answer. "Unfortunately," she said, "the average lifespan for a dog after being diagnosed with prostate cancer is seven or eight weeks."

"Seven or eight weeks?" I slowly repeated back to her, full of incredulity and distress that Ben's prognosis was this grim.

Her explanation erased what I had briefly assumed, "Prostate cancer is much more aggressive and difficult to treat in dogs than it is in humans."

I sat there shell-shocked. I walked into the clinic hoping to get some clarity on a lingering gastrointestinal problem. Thirty minutes later, I find out Ben has prostate cancer and that he has two months or less to live. With each unfolding revelation, the news was getting worse. I looked down at Ben and tried to think, but I couldn't.

We numbly walked out of the clinic into a cold and dark February night. We had been there about an hour. The world felt like it had come to a stop, but of course it hadn't. Life was carrying on around us despite what we had just found out. The mood in the car was beyond somber. We talked little and only about Ben—how much in disbelief we were, what the lab results might be, what we should do next, what a great dog he was. My mother kept saying, "That beautiful dog. What a shame."

* * *

I dropped my folks off at their house and drove home alone with Ben. My only desire after parking the car in the garage was to go straight to bed. For the first time in a long time, maybe my whole lifetime, I lost interest in everything.

Watch the late news? Who cares? Check email? Why? Call someone? For what?

My beloved Ben had terminal cancer, and nothing else mattered.

With Ben in his own bed right next to mine, I turned off the light, lay down, and in the pitch darkness, started to sob. My chest heaved; my stomach ached as if it had been punched. Being home made me feel worse. I felt like I was in the middle of a bad dream over at the clinic, but now in familiar surroundings—in my own room, in my own bed, Ben curled up there on his bed—it started to sink in that this was for real.

I got on my knees in bed with my forehead pressed hard against the mattress and pleaded with God for a miracle, that somehow, some way, the lab results would come back tomorrow afternoon showing that Ben had an inflamed prostate rather than prostate cancer. As hard as I tried, however, I couldn't make myself believe that was going to happen. I saw the look in the doctor's eyes when she gave us the news. I knew that she knew.

All through this ordeal with Ben, God hadn't answered our prayers the way we wanted. I had always heard that "God's ways are higher than our ways" and "He has a bigger and better plan," but that seemed of little comfort right now. I wasn't so naive as to believe that I was somehow excluded from the universal experience of pain, suffering, and death. I just felt a sickening sense that it was now our turn.

I went in and out of sleep the whole night. Two or three times, Ben nudged my arm with his nose to let me know he had to go outside. I now knew why, and it made me feel worse. The dawn of Friday, February 9 brought exhaustion rather than rejuvenation. Waiting for the lab results to come midafternoon only portended a bitter cup I did not want to drink.

Sure enough, the final verdict came with a phone call to my parents from the vet we had seen the previous night. Just as the doctor had suspected, the lab results confirmed that Ben had "prostatic carcinoma/adenocarcinoma."

There would be no miracle. Ben had prostate cancer. My mom hung up and immediately called me. I remember where I was standing—on my driveway just outside the garage. I had been futilely trying to go about my day but couldn't focus on anything for more than a few seconds before a wave of dread would rush in. My mom's voice was filled with despair as she relayed the lab results to me. She said the doctor would be referring us to the University of Minnesota Veterinary Medical Center for a second opinion and treatment options.

We didn't talk long. What was there to say when all hope seemed lost? Having never experienced this type of serious cancer with anyone in our family, we had just taken our first steps of descent into a dark valley, having no idea where the bottom would be.

This "Black Friday" neared its end with an email from my dad sent to the rest of our family and a few close friends about the bad news of the last twenty-four hours.

Friday, February 9

Ben has prostate cancer. We are devastated, as he is like a human family member to us. He is so wonderful. At eight-and-a-half years old, he seems so young to have this. It is especially devastating to David.

We will be talking with the University of Minnesota Vet Department oncologist to get some idea of the progression to expect. Ben has lost weight. He is now down to seventy-one pounds and is having trouble urinating and defecating. We have been told the prostate cancer will close down his ability to urinate and defecate in time.

We are very, very sad. He is such a friend and a gentleman. He has never been any trouble to us, always kind and very gentle.

So true, Dad. And yes, so devastating.

CHAPTER 11

WEIGHING OPTIONS

It was just hours after receiving confirmation that my beloved Ben was terminally ill, and yet I was still trying to process the doctor's words from the night before, "A dog will typically live seven or eight weeks after being diagnosed with prostate cancer."

That was what she said, but what I heard was far more personal, "In two months, you will no longer have Ben."

During the past month of trying to figure out what was wrong with Ben, I had been experiencing the gnawing feeling that comes from something unknown and potentially serious occupying the shelf of your brain like a big, heavy, unopened box. You try to live your life but the box sits there like an elephant, unavoidable and weighing you down.

Having the box opened and finding out the truth about Ben's condition did anything but relieve the vexing burden. As I began to reflect on losing Ben—how much I would miss him, what the road ahead might entail—the intermittent angst I had felt during the past month turned into a deep, interminable pain that would not go away.

I suppose I could have responded differently and been thankful for the eight great years I had with Ben. Or I could have counted it a blessing to have him for two more months. Some dog owners don't even get that when they lose their dogs. Their best buddy gets hit by a car, or maybe worse, stolen, and they are left forever wondering and worrying what became of him or her. Yes, the scenario could have been worse for me, but I wasn't seeing any silver linings at this point.

Instead, I immediately hunkered down into a kind of basic-functioning mode with one primary focus: to take care of Ben.

It seemed only right to stay by the side of my boy, the one who had always stayed by my side all those years, the one who had patiently lain by my desk while I worked, day after day, quietly waiting for me to finish so we could do something together. After observing his devotedness over the many months of writing a previous book, I could think of nothing more appropriate than to close the acknowledgments by writing, "All right, Ben, I'll take you for a walk now."

Ben needed much more than a walk now, and I was going to be there for him every step of the way. There would be no carrying on with life as usual while fitting in some care for him on the side. No, no. It was time for me to slow down, cut back, and attend to my boy.

That meant some of the work that I had been doing since coming off the tennis tour five years earlier—speaking engagements, writing a newspaper column, serving on the board of the United States Tennis Association, competing in the occasional "senior" tennis event—would have to take a backseat. Being single and self-employed, I was fortunately at a point in life where I could take this "time out" for Ben.

There was one work responsibility, however, that I would have to manage and that was the Saturday morning radio show that I produced and hosted. Having just received the bad news about

Ben on this Friday, I was in no state of mind to drive over to the studio the next morning and talk over the airwaves. What would I even say? An on-air, group-therapy, collective cry session was out of the question. I had no idea what would come out of my mouth or how I'd react to listeners calling in. This wound wasn't just raw; it was wide open.

And so I called the radio station late Friday night and asked them to play a previously aired program the next morning. I don't recall what program it was, and strangely enough, that Saturday doesn't even appear in the list of past programs. It's like the entire weekend was sucked into a big black hole. That's certainly how it felt anyway.

* * *

On Tuesday, just four days after finding out that Ben had prostate cancer, my parents and I drove Ben to the Animal Cancer Center at the University of Minnesota Veterinary Medical Center to consult with Dr. Mark Johnson, a PhD clinical professor at the University's College of Veterinary Medicine and a specialist in animal oncology.

Dr. Johnson ordered a wide range of tests on Ben: a physical exam of the prostate, blood work, urinalysis, X-rays, and a second ultrasound. The tests confirmed what we already knew—Ben had prostate cancer. But at least it hadn't spread.

From there, Dr. Johnson laid out three treatment options, explaining each in terms of effectiveness, side effects, and cost. They were surgery, chemotherapy, and radiation.

We were surprised to learn that surgery to remove all or part of Ben's prostate, something that is commonly and successfully done with men, is risky and not often recommended for dogs because of the different way the prostate surrounds the urinary tract of a dog. Because of the likelihood of creating further complications, we decided in fairly short order to not go down the prostate surgery road.

Dr. Johnson went on to tell us about the second option—chemotherapy. Much like chemotherapy for humans, Ben would have a potent drug fed into his bloodstream that is designed to kill cancer cells.

I immediately conjured up images of the side effects of chemo that I'd seen in humans and transferred them over to Ben. Dr. Johnson tempered my pessimism by saying that most dogs tolerate chemo better than humans. Fatigue and nausea were definite possibilities though.

I may have been focusing too much on the downsides of chemotherapy, but the upside didn't seem very good either. Dr. Johnson said that the average survival time for dogs with prostate cancer taking chemotherapy was three to five months. Three to five months? *Wow*, I thought, *that's not very much longer than the two months we were given if we do nothing at all.*

The third option that Dr. Johnson presented was radiation therapy, where a machine would shoot beams of radiation through Ben's abdomen to kill the tumor. Radiation had its own list of side effects, including the potential for damaging the healthy tissue and organs in the surrounding area. And the average survival time was similar to chemo—only three to four months.

The cost of any of the treatments would run into the thousands of dollars. I would have been willing to pay almost any price if I had confidence that Ben would be cured or at least have a year or more of good life. But to spend that much money only to have him die in a few months and suffer bad side effects along the way? That seemed like the worst option.

I was stuck, but at the same time, I couldn't bear the thought of doing nothing to slow down the disease. It just wasn't in my nature to stand by while the cancer progressively took over his body.

We left the Vet Med Center facing the dilemma of doing something to solve a problem that might end up creating a bigger problem. It had almost been two weeks since Ben's diagnosis, and I needed to make a decision soon. The cancer wasn't standing still while I deliberated about the best course of treatment. I searched and searched online for anything related to canine prostate cancer, putting "treatment for dog with prostate cancer" into my computer's search engine dozens of times, digging many pages down.

In all my investigation, there was one thing I had missed. A vet named Dr. Michael Rivers was conducting research on prostate cancer in humans and dogs with the goal of finding a cure. Brodie had come across his work while doing some of her own online searching and emailed me his information, thinking I might want to talk with him about Ben's case.

I certainly did. Prostate cancer was so rare in dogs that it was difficult to find anyone anywhere who specialized in this particular kind of cancer. Not only did I want to speak with Dr. Rivers, but I wanted to speak with him soon before making any treatment decisions for Ben.

I did a background check on Dr. Rivers. He had quite the credentials, even beyond his DVM and PhD degrees. He was a professor of oncology at a well-known university's veterinary school and was one of the scientists selected by the National Cancer Institute to develop the prostate cancer research agenda for the United States. I figured the man must know his stuff.

In my first conversation with Dr. Rivers, it came across loud and clear that he was a visionary who was passionate about his work. This guy lived, slept, and breathed finding a cure for cancer. He listened closely as I described Ben's case history and the treatment options I was considering. While not completely opposed to chemotherapy and radiation, he felt both would be seen as roughshod methods of treating cancer twenty years into the future, sort of like poisoning the whole pond to remove one invasive species. He surmised that there had to be a better way, and his lifework was to discover it.

For the previous several years, he had been directing a trial study on a treatment for prostate cancer. Tumor cells grown in mice were put into tiny gel capsules—what I call microseeds— and surgically placed around the cancerous tumor inside a dog. The idea was that the dog's system would react to and kill off the microseeds, and in so doing, shrink the real cancerous tumor as well.

It sounded sorta out there, but at the same time, I wasn't completely thrown off by the concept. My brother was a medical doctor who performed a treatment for chronic pain in which a natural solution was injected at the site of the injury, causing a localized reaction and stimulating the body to heal itself. It was like starting a controlled burn to put out the bigger fire.

I was intrigued by the microseed procedure but reticent about placing Ben in a trial study. I know every medical advance starts this way, but I didn't want Ben to be the guinea pig, so to speak. I'm not a risktaker by nature, especially when it comes to something as important to me as Ben. But, with my back against the wall, I felt I needed to consider all the options.

Dr. Rivers told me that he had performed the microseed procedure on about a dozen dogs with prostate cancer and that a handful did well enough that the procedure was repeated in five months, with some of them living up to a year or more.

A year or more? This definitely got my attention, as it was quite a bit longer than the average survival times for chemotherapy or radiation.

The upside sounded great, but what about the downside? I'd like to think Ben would be Dr. Rivers' best-ever patient, but what if he wasn't? How long did the average dog live and with what quality of life?

Dr. Rivers said most of the dogs in the study lived about six months after diagnosis, and surprisingly, he reported the side effects were pretty minimal—maybe some malaise or fever. He said recovering from the one-hour surgery was the biggest risk, and that really wasn't much risk at all.

I pressed him further, asking about any dogs that hadn't done well. He said there was one dog who had reacted poorly and died within weeks, but he didn't know exactly why, considering most dogs had little trouble tolerating the microseeds.

I knew I was entering medical no-man's land, caught between this-generation and next-generation medicine. Here I had called Dr. Rivers to get a second opinion about chemo and radiation, and now I felt like I needed to get a second opinion on Dr. Rivers' second opinion.

And so, in a follow-up appointment with Dr. Johnson at the University of Minnesota a few days later, I brought up the microseed procedure. He was only vaguely aware of it and seemed a little skeptical. His recommendation stayed the same as the week before—go with a combination treatment of chemotherapy and an anti-inflammatory medication that Ben was already taking.

Over the next couple days, I thought about what to do, prayed about what to do, and talked it over with my parents. Making a big decision like this was hard enough; feeling the pressure to make it quickly made it even more difficult.

I decided to go mainstream. Even though there seemed to be a greater likelihood of side effects with chemotherapy, there was also much more data to show its effectiveness.

And so late on Friday, February 23, two weeks to the day after receiving word that Ben had prostate cancer, I called the Animal Cancer Center to prepay for the first dose of chemotherapy and set up an appointment to have it given to Ben on Monday morning. I was reluctant, but I couldn't let any more days slip away.

All weekend I wrestled with it and so did my mom. Neither of us could get around the fear of making him even more sick. Ben was always super-sensitive about being given any sort of medicine. For goodness sake, he would slink away whenever I pulled out the little bottle of ear cleanser. How on earth was he going to get through four or five chemotherapy treatments without being completely waylaid?

By the time Monday morning dawned, I had talked myself out of it. I just couldn't bring myself to take Ben in. I called the University Animal Cancer Center and cancelled the appointment.

In doing so, however, I had just reduced my options. Now it was either the microseed surgery or nothing at all.

I still couldn't accept doing nothing, and so I phoned Dr. Rivers again to drill down deeper into what his procedure would entail, conferencing my parents in on the call.

Dr. Rivers said he could do the microseed surgery on Ben later in the week on Friday, at a veterinary hospital in Chicago. My parents and I would drive Ben from Minneapolis to Chicago on Thursday, meet with Dr. Rivers, and if all went well with the surgery on Friday morning, we would bring Ben home to Minneapolis on Sunday. Since the trial study was funded by the cancer foundation, there would be no charge for the surgery and post-op care. We would just need to take Ben to our own vet for monthly check-ups and blood tests and send the results to Dr. Rivers. If Ben responded well and a follow-up ultrasound showed the tumor was shrinking, a second microseed surgery would be considered in five months.

We finished the call and my parents and I stayed on the line to discuss it further amongst ourselves. My dad and I were mostly favorable. My mom? Not so much. She didn't like any of the treatment options—microseeds, chemo, radiation. But she wasn't adamant that we do nothing either.

I went to bed facing another night of sleepless deliberation. And yet in the midst of all my laboring, I saw a glimmer of hope with the microseed surgery. There was the upside potential of a longer life expectancy, and there was the lack of downside with side effects. It was right there on the trial study consent form, "The side effects seen most often with this procedure involve a mild transient fever and malaise. These side effects usually last for less than twenty-four hours and generally do not require intervention."

Sometime that night I made the decision. I woke up and called my parents to say that I thought we should take Ben to Chicago. "The worst thing that will happen is that the microseeds won't work," I reassured them and myself. "At least we will have done something to try to help Ben."

CHAPTER 12

ROAD TRIP

Two days later, Ben slept quietly in the backseat during the seven-hour drive from Minneapolis to Chicago. It was the first day of March, and the dirty snow along the freeway in Minnesota gradually disappeared as we traveled southeast across Wisconsin.

Arriving later in the afternoon, we set our eyes upon Dr. Rivers for the first time in an exam room at an animal hospital outside the city. Joining him was Dr. Julie Harris, a vet in her thirties who practiced at the clinic and collaborated with Dr. Rivers when he came to town for surgery. They presented a professional and personable team—Dr. Rivers, intelligent, driven, and robust in his late forties, and Dr. Harris, bright, amiable, and caring.

Dr. Rivers walked us through every aspect of the microseed procedure, pre-op to post-op, answering our each and every question from how many of the tiny microseeds would be implanted in Ben's abdomen (hundreds) to how we would know if they were working to shrink the tumor (ultrasound). He encouraged us by saying that Ben was the ideal candidate to benefit from the procedure because his cancer hadn't spread.

After years of encountering all manner of "medical experts" attempting to push their latest and greatest treatment on a pro athlete, my parents and I had developed finely tuned quackery meters. Dr. Rivers may have come across a little too confident for our tastes, but there was nothing here to suggest that we were entering the snake oil realm.

The one seemingly minor detail that was our biggest objection had to do with Dr. Rivers wanting Ben kept overnight at the hospital in order to be monitored and ready for surgery the following morning. We knew that Ben would not take well to a vet clinic sleepover and suggested that Ben stay with us at the hotel. Both doctors preferred otherwise, however, and as it didn't seem like a hill to die on, we decided to take Ben to our hotel until the time eventually came to take him over to the clinic for the night.

Only one problem: Ben didn't want to go. I had heard about dog premonitions—like when your dog snarls at the man selling something at the door and then you find out later that the guy was actually casing homes to rob in the neighborhood. But I had never experienced any dog premonitions with Ben. He had quite the vocabulary, but surely he hadn't picked up on the doctor's comment in the exam room about staying overnight at the clinic. For all Ben knew, I was calling him off the couch of the hotel room to go outside for a walk. But no, he knew something was up.

Something snapped within my mother when she saw that Ben didn't want to leave. It was like a dam had broken, and she suddenly emoted all that she had been holding inside: she didn't like the idea of the microseeds, she didn't care for Dr. Rivers, and she wanted to chuck the whole thing and drive home as soon as possible. It was almost ten o'clock in the evening and a cold rain was falling outside. I'm not sure if she meant right then or in the morning, but if I had to guess, she probably meant right then.

An emotional tug of war ensued in the hotel room—my mother expressing her every fear, and my father and I trying to calm her down and reassure her that we were making the best decision with the least amount of risk, and that we shouldn't back out now just because Ben didn't want to leave the room. And besides, "We have come all this way to do something to help Ben."

She wasn't persuaded. And yet she wasn't going to lie on the train tracks to keep us from taking Ben to the hospital. A washing of the hands was taking place. My mom was basically telling us, "Do what you will, but I'm against this."

My dad and I said little as we drove Ben to the hospital.

At this hour of the night, the clinic was deserted except for a few night staff who took care of the pets being boarded overnight and those coming in after-hours for emergencies. Ben was unsettled as we waited in the lobby. He kept standing up on his hind legs to put his front legs on me, pleading not to leave him there. How on earth did he know?

I kneeled down on the hard floor next to Ben. I talked softly to him, told him how much of a good boy he was, and stroked him reassuringly. Half a minute later, the dreaded moment came to turn his leash over to the staff person. She led Ben toward the door that went to the back. Ben kept turning his head to look at me. He didn't want to go, but he was too noble to make a scene. They disappeared behind the door, and my dad and I walked silently to the car. I was glad my mother hadn't seen any of this. I felt horrible, like I had just betrayed the one who had always trusted me.

* * *

With the surgery scheduled for 9:00 a.m., we decided that it would be better for Ben if we didn't visit him beforehand and get his hopes up, only to have to disappoint him again by leaving. But we did arrive at the hospital in advance of the surgery for a short pre-op meeting with Dr. Rivers and Dr. Harris. The surgery would be fairly straightforward, taking about an hour.

After the meeting, my parents and I went out to the lobby to wait and settled into some chairs in the corner of the room. Just as when Ben had his first ultrasound, we leaned in toward each other and I quietly prayed that the surgery would go well and be successful. Afterward my mom took out her well-worn Bible. She read it every day and always in trying moments, such as when my dad went in for each of his three open-heart surgeries. She may have been stressed, but she knew where her source of strength lay. I had brought a pocket Bible myself and read a few passages from the book of Psalms but was finding it hard to concentrate. My mind kept wandering into the operating room to think about what was happening to Ben.

I was hoping that time would hurry along, but the hands on the large clock on the wall behind the front desk appeared resistant to moving. An hour came and went, and then another fifteen minutes, and we hadn't heard a thing. *What is taking so long?* I nervously wondered. Finally an assistant came through the door to tell us that they were almost finished.

We met with Dr. Rivers shortly after the surgery, and he said that other than taking a little longer than anticipated, everything had gone according to plan. Now it was a matter of Ben recuperating from the operation for a few days and then waiting to see what effect the microseeds would have on his tumor. Dr. Rivers said he would be heading home in the afternoon but that Dr. Harris would be around to monitor Ben all weekend. We, of course, wanted to see Ben right away but couldn't because he needed time to recover.

Later in the day we returned to find Ben in his kennel looking groggy and down. It hurt to see him in such a state. I opened the metal gate and got down next to him on the ground. A stark contrast took shape in my mind. Here I was, on the cold, hard floor of a small cement block kennel in an animal hospital hundreds of miles from home, petting my wonderful dog who was just hanging on after surgery. Memories flooded in from all the times Ben and I had spent together over the years—on the lake, at the cabin, in the fields, in the woods, at home. All that seemed a world away now, completely unrelated to what I was experiencing in this moment. *Is this the same dog? Am I the same person? Is this even the same life?*

By Sunday afternoon, after what seemed like the longest of weekends, one in which we had done little more than wait, eat, sleep, and visit Ben, he was ready to be released from the hospital and make the drive home. We had a final conversation with Dr. Harris and said our good-byes to her and the clinic staff, all of whom had gone above and beyond in their care and concern for Ben and us. They had made a trying time a little more tolerable.

The winter sun was bright as I walked Ben across the parking lot to our car. He moved slowly and deliberately, as if holding back a queasy stomach. I gently lifted him into the backseat and then got in next to him. As we drove from suburban streets to rural interstate, dusk and then darkness gradually enveloped the countryside. It had been a long, hard weekend, and I was beyond glad to be heading home. I'm sure Ben felt the same.

It was late by the time we arrived at my parents' house. I decided to stay the night in their extra room downstairs rather than drive the additional fifteen minutes to my own house. It wasn't the late hour that kept me from going home, however. Rather, after all we'd been through, it didn't feel right to immediately return to our regular routines of Ben and me at my house and my parents at theirs.

No, something inside told me that we needed to be close together now, to support Ben, to support each other.

* * *

After returning home on the first Sunday in March, we experienced a few days of relative quiet as Ben regained some strength following the surgery. But that didn't last long. I was soon in daily phone contact with Dr. Harris, giving her updates and asking why Ben wasn't bouncing back. His appetite was minimal, his mood down, and he was throwing up on occasion.

Two weeks to the day after Ben's surgery, we took him to our local vet to have his stitches removed and to consult with Dr. Logan, the part-time vet who had scheduled Ben's first ultrasound when his cancer was discovered. Was it the micro-seeds that were causing Ben's malaise? Stomach ulcers from the anti-inflammatory medication? The cancer spreading? Something else? Whatever it was, Ben was going the wrong direction. And now I was struggling to get him to eat anything.

A critical turning point takes place when a dog stops eating. In retrospect, I wish I had proceeded differently from here on out, but my protective instinct was to do whatever I could to help Ben. I could see him losing weight and knew he would only get worse if he didn't eat. What I didn't realize is that when a dog stops eating, he's trying to tell you something. Something I did not want to hear.

I was still thinking Ben was in a recovery rut from the surgery and that he'd right himself any day now. *He just needs to get over the hump*, I tried to encourage myself.

Two days later on Sunday, I drove to church in the morning with Ben in the back of the car, intending to take him over to my parents' house in the afternoon. My parents and I walked over to the car after the service, and upon opening the rear cargo door, were collectively shocked to find Ben lying there looking dazed and sick. We immediately took him to the twenty-four-hour emergency vet hospital that was only a couple miles away.

The emergency clinic took a blood sample from Ben and discovered that his kidney values were dangerously outside normal. A urine test showed a potential infection. An IV was attached to Ben to get him nourishment and fluids, and various medications were given to address his nausea and urinary tract infection. He would need to stay at the emergency vet hospital for two days. I felt overwhelmed and depressed.

Thankfully, Ben had recovered enough by Tuesday to be released. It was a relief to pick him up and drive him to familiar surroundings at my parents' house. We decided it was best to keep him in one place now and their house was the logical choice. It would be easier for me to stay there to give Ben the kind of care he needed with some backup support.

Nearly two weeks passed, and it was April 1, Palm Sunday, the start of Easter week. We went to church in the morning, and after returning home, my mom took Ben out for a short walk. She returned dejected. Ben had thrown up again. The recurring vomiting had become a real problem. It was difficult enough to get any nourishment in him, let alone have him keep it down.

That evening, instead of yet another night of sleeping on my parents' dining room floor with Ben curled up next to me, I moved out of the main house to a room above their detached garage. The room was dusty and cold, but it had one thing I really wanted—a bed. Plus, with fewer stairs than the main house, it would be easier to let Ben outside during the night.

When I was growing up, this room over the garage served as part game room, part storage area and didn't get much use. That is, until my parents secretly remodeled the room when I was away for a series of tennis tournaments late one spring. I remember arriving home from Wimbledon in early July and my parents leading me out to what I thought was the same old storage area. Instead, the room had been beautifully transformed into a large studio, complete with bed, desk, couch, fridge, closets, carpeting, and bathroom. Pictures and memorabilia from all my years growing up and playing tennis hung on the walls. It was like receiving that one special Christmas gift you never forget, in the summer, no less!

Through no intention of my own, I lived only one year in the room. My brother John, who was also living at my parents' house at the time, persuaded me to go in with him on a rustic home about ten minutes away. It was a great location, with big views of the lake and dramatic sunsets. But barely a year after moving in, John was engaged, married, and moved out, leaving me at age twenty-two to be on my own in a home that I would never have bought if it hadn't been for his urging. There was no going back to Dad and Mom's now. I would live alone in that house for the next six years—that is, until a cute little Labrador puppy joined me . . . named Ben.

There was something strange about being back in my old room above my parents' garage fifteen years after I had moved out, especially having Ben there with me. The major stages of my life seemed to be intersecting all at once in this room. There was the childhood picture of me playing in the yard with those crazy Siberian huskies. There were trophies from teenage tennis victories adorning the shelves. There was the surfboard from my high school years in Florida hanging above the couch. There were books and papers on the desk from my time at Stanford, and a closetful of clothes from an obviously different fashion era. And there were also a few souvenirs displayed around the room from my first two years on the pro tour—a deerskin from South Africa, a boomerang from Australia, and a Russian military hat from Moscow.

The early years of my life surrounded me, and yet there was not one thing about Ben, except for him lying there next to me. It struck me how Ben had no impact on this part of my life, but that my last eight-and-a-half years had been dominated by his presence. If I drove a short distance to my own home, Ben was everywhere: pictures on the walls of Ben and me doing something or other and endless dog paraphernalia scattered about—dishes and beds, retrieving dummies, leashes, collars, and toys. It was all Ben, all over.

Ben had become such a strong presence in my life that the pre-Ben era in my old room at my parents' seemed so way-back-then. I wish I could have avoided my next thought, but I couldn't. My current era with Ben was coming to an end and would seem so way-back-then someday as well. A stream of melancholy ran through me as I reflected on that coming reality.

I dreaded that I would soon be left with only some pictures and fading memories or maybe a memento or two like Ben's orange hunting collar or the blue ribbon he had won in a retrieving contest. But what could I do about it? Ben had terminal cancer. He was going the way of all living things, and I was powerless to stop it. Soon I would be left to somehow deal with his loss and go on, and I had no idea how I was going to do that.

* * *

In the middle of the night, I was awakened by Ben throwing up next to my bed. I let him out while I cleaned up and then walked over to the window to watch him in the yard. He stood there in the dark, thin, weak, and rickety. For the first time throughout this whole ordeal, a line was crossed in my mind. Previously, I was always thinking about what I needed to do next to keep Ben going; now, I started to think about when was the right time to put him down.

I knew I would seek counsel from my family and vet. But I also knew that I needed to make the final decision—and it had to be a decision I would not regret.

For one person, the decision is made when his dog stops eating. For another, it may be when her dog loses bladder control. Still others make the call shortly after a terminal diagnosis. Whatever the circumstances, the decision is mostly based on saving the dog from further suffering . . . or saving the owner from the high costs of advanced treatments. Others are willing to travel much farther down the road. That may be all the way until "nature takes its course."

Each situation has its own unique set of circumstances, and quality of life for dog and owner will be defined and measured differently by different people. It's easy to draw nice straight lines and say, "This is what I would do." Easy, that is, until you find yourself in the middle of your own excruciating battle between mind and emotion.

That is precisely where I found myself with Ben. I was hoping that the right time would be obvious to me. I didn't want to put him down one day too early or one day too late. I'm sure some will think that I waited too long, while others, that I should have held on longer. But in the end, the one thing I have never regretted with Ben was when and how I said good-bye.

CHAPTER 13

DARKEST DAY

The next day was Monday, April 2, and the gloomy weather outside matched the mood inside with my parents and me. It was another day spent hoping Ben would swallow a little pureed food that I would dab on his tongue from a feeding syringe and talking on the phone with Dr. Harris in Chicago and Dr. Logan in Minneapolis. For the last couple weeks, both vets had been collaborating on Ben's case and so I felt we were getting well-reasoned advice. Nevertheless, I went to bed that night in the room over my parents' garage knowing Ben was in a touch-and-go situation.

There were no major problems during the night besides the usual three or four nudges to let him outside. In the morning, I helped him up into my bed, where he nestled in and went to sleep. I lay there on my side, deep in thought with my arm draped over him and my body contoured around him. Twenty minutes later, we got up and walked across the driveway and into the main house.

Ben followed me down the hallway into my parents' bedroom where my mom was reading the newspaper. I gave her a short update on how Ben had done during the night and then lifted him into their bed before heading to the kitchen to prepare some food and medications for him.

Seeing me return with the feeding syringe, Ben got his usual "Do I really have to?" expression on his face. He didn't like being fed this way, and I'm sure he wasn't even hungry. I understood, and it hurt to make him do something he didn't want to do, especially with the way he was feeling.

I left Ben to sleep while I went back out to the kitchen to make breakfast for myself. In his healthy days, Ben would have been right there in a flash, begging at the first sound of life in the kitchen. Those days were a distant memory now.

Ben eventually appeared in the living room outside the kitchen as I was washing dishes. Considering his frail condition, I was surprised that he had gotten himself down out of the bed. But there he was, standing in the middle of the room, looking a little unsteady.

Before heading into the dining room to do some work, I led Ben over to the end of the couch in the corner of the living room so that he could take a nap in his favorite spot. Ben loved this little perch where he could rest his head on the armrest and take in the whole scene on the bay in front of my parents' home. All year long, the south sun beamed through the large picture windows, and there was always something for Ben to watch: ducks, geese, and boats trolling about in the summer, and fishermen boring holes through the ice and folks skating or snowshoeing in the winter.

It was about ten o'clock in the morning by the time I walked into the dining room to turn on my laptop. With all that had been taking place since Ben's diagnosis just over seven weeks before, I had been in minimum-work mode. I was doing just enough to prep for my Saturday radio show and that was about all. It was probably good that I had some work responsibilities to divert my mind away from Ben for an hour here and there, but as for generating new business or answering every email . . . sorry, my heart was elsewhere.

All was quiet in the house. The phone wasn't ringing. My parents were in other rooms. Ben was asleep on the couch. It seemed like Tuesday, April 3 was just going to be another day of watch-and-wait, looking after Ben.

I hadn't been at the dining room table for long—maybe twenty or thirty minutes—when the silence was broken by Ben throwing up in the next room. Just hearing him caused me to close my eyes and drop my head in discouragement. After all the effort to feed him that morning, he had already thrown up.

Deep, hard thoughts were going through my mind as I went into the kitchen to get a rag to wipe things up. I was confounded and depressed. *Why can't he keep his food down?* I asked myself in frustration.

I knew this vomiting must be hard on him but I didn't know what to do about it. *Maybe I should call . . .*

I was halfway through the thought when all of a sudden Ben went into a full-body spasm on the couch like he was having a seizure. A literal pulsation of fear gripped me. I stood there frozen, not knowing what was going on or what to do.

The episode lasted less than a minute. I quickly got down next to him and could see in his eyes that he was as alarmed as I was. I carefully rolled him onto his side, making long strokes from his head down to his back legs to reassure him that I was there and he was going to be all right. Without lifting his head, he responded with a few thumps of his tail against the cushion, as if trying to reassure me that he was fine. That was just like Ben—trying to make me feel better.

After a couple minutes when Ben's body began to relax, I went to find my parents to tell them what had happened. They rushed into the living room, and we all stood there looking at Ben with grave concern etched on our faces.

I immediately called Dr. Logan. She offered several possible explanations: it could be an electrolyte imbalance from vomiting, it could be the shutting down of an internal organ from the cancer . . . or it could be something entirely unknown. Whatever it was, she conveyed in so many words that this was a very negative turn of events. She went on to say that we could take Ben over to the emergency vet hospital, but I didn't think he was in any condition to be transported anywhere at this point. We hung up, deciding that I would monitor Ben for a while and then call her back.

It wasn't long before I was calling her back. Just a half hour passed when Ben relapsed into a similar seizure-like episode on the couch. This time my parents were in the room, and we watched in helpless distress as Ben went into another spasm. And then just as quickly as it started, it stopped.

Witnessing Ben fail so precipitously did something to me beyond imprinting an indelible image on my mind. It pushed me to a place where I needed to go; a place, though, where I never wanted to be. It forced me to come to terms with the fact that his body was shutting down and that I could not and would not allow my beloved Ben to endure more of this.

One thing I had decided was that I would not take Ben into a vet clinic to put him down. I couldn't bear the thought of walking him out of the house for the last time, driving him in the car for the last time, walking him into the exam room for the last time, watching him be put to sleep, and then driving home alone without him.

Some choose to turn over the leash and not be there — and

there's nothing wrong with that—but as for me, I knew I had to be there with him until the very end and "there" would be a place where he and we felt comfortable. We were at that place right now.

I called Dr. Logan back. She was not at work but had another commitment that kept her from coming over right away to evaluate Ben. I say "evaluate" because I didn't want to make a final decision with Ben until I had received an in-person, professional opinion, which Dr. Logan would provide.

It was a long, hard wait. I returned to the living room and gazed out the big picture windows for a moment. It was a wretched day. The clouds were gray and heavy and seemed to be hovering just above the trees. A wet April snow was falling in a vain attempt to cover the earth's winter wounds.

Ben had been in the house all morning, and I thought he might need to go outside. I didn't know whether he could stand or walk or whether I'd have to carry him. To my surprise, when I went over to the couch, he tried to get down on his own. I let him, but as soon his paws touched the hardwood floors, his back legs gave way.

There didn't seem to be any chance of his making it the fifteen feet over to the door, but that didn't keep him from trying. He somehow regained his balance and took a few wobbly steps toward the door before he had to stop and catch himself from giving way again.

I was standing at the couch silently looking on. He turned his head back to look at me and began to wag his tail, as if embarrassed that I had to see him like this. I couldn't take it anymore. I walked over and gathered him into my arms and carried him out the door and down the stairs to the yard.

The weather outside felt as raw as it looked. It was cold and damp with big wet flakes coming down. I carefully put Ben on the ground, thinking that he might do a little better on the grass than on the hardwood floors. He did, but not by much. I watched him closely, carefully analyzing his every move and demeanor as he struggled to take a few steps before eventually squatting down to urinate a few drops.

Ben was hardly able to function. I could see it with my eyes and feel it in the deepest part of my being. It was in this moment, barring some recommendation to the contrary from Dr. Logan, that I decided that this day would be our last together. Today—just today, not yesterday—Ben's quality of life had deteriorated below what was acceptable to me for my noble and beloved dog. I carried him back into the house and laid him down in his favorite spot on the couch overlooking the bay.

* * *

Dr. Logan drove her minivan up the driveway around two-thirty that afternoon and walked up the stairs into the living room with a small duffle bag of veterinary gear. I updated her on Ben's condition as she began to examine him. Ben lay quietly on the couch and hardly seemed to notice as Dr. Logan sat next to him, checking his eyes, gums, breathing, and pulse.

There was a pregnant silence in the room for the five or so minutes it took her to assess Ben. The mood was heavy and serious. My parents and I sat there watching and wondering what her conclusions would be.

After finishing the exam, Dr. Logan turned to us and reported that Ben's heart rate did not match his pulse rate, which she thought could be the result of his heart stopping during one of his seizure episodes earlier in the day. Whatever the cause, Dr.

Logan's assessment was that Ben had reached a point where too many things were going wrong and that his quality of life had been reduced such that we should consider putting him down.

Her recommendation didn't send me reeling, probably because I had come to the same conclusion an hour or so earlier. But still, hearing these words from someone in the same room who could actually carry out what she was suggesting was a harsh reality.

We discussed other options, but there just weren't any that I was willing to put Ben through. An obvious one was to take Ben over to the emergency vet hospital. But in his condition? And to stay overnight—and perhaps die—in a place he disliked? No way.

Another was to wait and see how Ben did over the next day or so. When he could hardly stand? When he was having seizures? When I had no real means of getting him to eat or drink?

No, we were out of options, at least acceptable ones.

I then asked Dr. Logan a simple question, "What would you do if Ben were your dog?"

Dr. Logan hesitated for a few moments, clearly trying to consider what she'd do if Ben were her dog. Although she hadn't been Ben's vet for most of his life, she was the one who had examined him and arranged that first ultrasound back in early February when his cancer was discovered. She was the one we had been in contact with most regularly since then. She was the one, along with Dr. Harris in Chicago, who had gone the extra mile and taken special interest in Ben and us. Whatever her counsel, we would be taking it very seriously.

She answered as if thinking out loud, touching on several of the problems Ben was experiencing, and how these were the result of a cascading effect where one complication turns into another. She then concluded with a sympathetic tone that, considering Ben's deteriorated quality of life, if Ben were her dog, she would probably put him down. We knew that she had given us an honest answer. The "probably," I gathered, was for our benefit, so that we would feel some latitude to make a different decision.

I asked her what the process would be. She said she would inject a sedative into Ben to make him drowsy, followed by a dose of sodium pentothal to stop his heart. She assured me that he would feel no pain and would simply "go to sleep" as the euphemism implies.

I didn't doubt her, but the gravity of taking a deliberate action to end Ben's life when he was lying there alive on the couch was inexpressibly hard to contemplate.

Dr. Logan went out to her car to give us some time alone to discuss the decision. My brother Mark, soon joined us, having driven over from his medical clinic. Mark wanted to be there for us in our most difficult moment and prayed aloud for wisdom, for strength, for help.

Twenty minutes or more passed and Dr. Logan was still waiting in her car. The delay wasn't so much about "Should we or shouldn't we?" as much as coming to terms with the impending reality of life without Ben. This was the bitter cup that none of us wanted to drink.

Dr. Logan eventually came to the door and said that while she didn't want to rush us, she had another appointment and could come back in the evening if we wanted more time. More time wasn't our problem. We knew what we had to do; we knew what the best decision was, at least for Ben. The real problem was saying good-bye for the final time to this wonderful dog who had been such a beloved member of our family and brought such joy to our lives.

Ben was still resting quietly at the end of the couch. Over the last hour I kept looking at him, thinking, *He seems to be doing better now; he hasn't had a seizure in a few hours; maybe I should wait a little longer.*

I knew deep down that a few more hours wasn't going to help. This was the right time, and my parents realized it as well. There was no dissension among us, but the final decision had to be mine.

I don't recall exactly what I said or how I even got the words out, but I somehow communicated to Dr. Logan that we wanted her to put Ben down.

Dr. Logan responded empathetically, assuring us that she also thought that this was the best decision for Ben in his failing condition.

Holding a few medical items, she made her way to the couch and sat down next to Ben's rear legs. I went over as well and kneeled on the floor next to his head. Ben was lying on his side, nodding in and out of sleep. Despite his thin body, his face still had that look of serenity and nobility that had always characterized him. I put my arm around him, buried my head into his neck, and closed my eyes, trying to cherish the last remaining moments with my wonderful dog. I whispered through his coat how much I loved him and what a good boy he was.

I continued to hold on to Ben as Dr. Logan injected the sedative into his left rear leg. Ben didn't flinch. It would take a minute or two for the sedative to take effect.

The room was completely silent. My mother sat a few feet away in her chair by the window. My dad was an equal distance away in his recliner. Mark stood across the room. All of them were beyond somber.

Dr. Logan got out the second syringe with the sodium pentothal.

I continued to stroke Ben. He didn't appear to be acting any differently after the sedative. Maybe that was because he had already been going in and out of sleep.

This would be my final moment with Ben. I don't know what I was expecting, but all my years with him didn't flash across my mind. I didn't think back to the myriad of memories and wonderful times. I only felt a chest-gripping sorrow.

Dr. Logan found a suitable vein in his leg and slowly injected the lethal solution. While she was doing so, Ben, who had been still throughout the entire process, lifted his head to look toward his rear leg.

Thinking something was going wrong, I turned to Dr. Logan and exclaimed, "What is happening?!" The anxiety inside of me overflowed, transporting me to a state of mind where I had never been. Her reply was short and accurate, "David, you're in shock." Before I could respond, Ben turned his head back and placed it down on the pillow and closed his eyes. After removing the needle, she put on her stethoscope to listen to Ben's heart. It didn't take more than ten or fifteen seconds for her to say quietly, "His heart has stopped—he's gone."

I heard her. I believed her. But I still continued to make long strokes from Ben's head down his side. His body lay there exactly the same as it had a minute ago. Only now, life had left him. Where did my Ben go? I could not stir him or wake him up. I could not get a response from his beautiful brown eyes.

It was 3:45 p.m. on Tuesday, the third day of April, and my life with Ben had come to an end.

CHAPTER 14

AFTERSHOCK

For several minutes, we all remained frozen in our respective positions in the living room, staring at nothing and deep in reflection. The only sound that broke the silence was the short, gasping breaths of my mother. "That wonderful dog," she tearfully and repeatedly lamented. My dad sat in his chair, breaking down as well. Both of them loved Ben as much as I. Mark came over to me and put his hand on my shoulder. I hadn't moved from beside the couch, slumped over with my head down and hand still on Ben.

We had just lost a beloved member of our family. A dog, yes, but a loved one indeed.

Fifteen minutes passed, and Dr. Logan needed to leave for an appointment. She would be taking Ben's body to her clinic in order to be transported to Dr. Harris in Chicago, where an autopsy would be performed as part of the trial study. After the autopsy, his body would be cremated and the ashes sent back to us in Minnesota.

Dr. Logan asked me if I would be willing to carry Ben's body out to her car. There was no question. I lifted his lifeless form off the couch and cradled him across my chest as I walked through the living room, down the stairs, out the door, to the rear of her minivan. I carefully laid him in the back and closed the door.

If any day in my entire life could be described as surreal, this was it. I did not wake up in the morning expecting that I'd be standing in the driveway later in the afternoon, having just placed Ben's body in the back of Dr. Logan's car. I did not foresee that I would watch Ben seize up, and a couple hours later, see him being put down. I never, ever imagined when I got up this morning what I would see, feel, and experience.

But this was no dream. I stood there in the driveway on this awful day and embraced Dr. Logan, thanking her for all she'd done. She had gone above and beyond for us, not just on this day, but consistently throughout the previous seven-and-a-half weeks. I would have wanted no one but her to put Ben down. She had been professional, and just as important, she had been personable.

But there she was backing down the driveway and heading up the street with the body of my beloved Ben in the back of her van. I had turned over Ben's leash for good this time. He would not be coming back through the door.

I walked slowly into the house, went upstairs into the living room, and sat in the same spot where Ben had been lying on the couch. My parents and Mark were still in the room. A dam inside me broke all at once. I began to sob uncontrollably, crying as I had never cried in all my life. I don't cry often, and hadn't done so since the days surrounding Ben's cancer diagnosis back in February. But now I couldn't stop. Neither could my dad and my mom. We went on for an hour, just weeping. A horrible ache gripped my stomach and chest. Benjamin, the son of my right hand, was now the son of my sorrow.

A couple hours passed and Mark left for home. My mom made dinner and we sat in the living room, eating in a kind of stupor.

Normally we would have watched the news or something on TV, but nothing happening in the world seemed of any consequence. We could only think about Ben.

Eventually the clock said it was getting near bedtime, but how on earth was I going to sleep? After what happened today? With Ben not by my bed for the first time in nearly nine years?

I couldn't imagine going to bed in the room over the garage where I had spent the previous night with Ben. But I was in no condition to go back to my house alone either. My parents' spare bedroom downstairs was where I would sleep tonight . . . or at least attempt to do so.

Before heading downstairs, I thought I should send a short email to the rest of my family and a few close friends to let them know about Ben. They had been supporting us along the way, and they deserved to know sooner rather than later.

I went into the dining room and sat down at the round table in front of my laptop. My parents had already retreated to their bedroom for the night, and the house was dark except for the soft light coming down from the old stained-glass lamp hanging above my head.

What was I to say in a moment like this? The last three months, and especially the last two, had been an intensely painful and personal travail for my parents and me, and although the rest of my family and Brodie and a few others were aware of what was taking place, they hadn't been on the inside to see Ben's decline close-up or the depth of angst that we were experiencing.

With the hour late and my emotions raw, I decided it wasn't the right time to go into much detail about the events of the day. I would keep things short and to the point.

Before I could put any words on the page, I noticed that there was an email from Mark in my inbox. It was addressed to our parents and me.

David, Dad, and Mom:

At 3:45 p.m. today, Ben peacefully left your lives and all of us who knew and loved him.

It is the most difficult thing you have ever had to do— but it was the right thing to do and the right time to do it. Ben did not need nor did he want (if he could've spoken, and he most certainly did with his soft brown eyes) to endure his suffering any longer. He disliked any physical or verbal discomfort to the same degree that he loved you three and just being with David wherever he went. I felt it a privilege to be able to help share and bear your burdens today as a brother and son. I always am grateful to God for allowing me to be at Granny's side and hold her hand as she died. It was the same today. Only this time I was privileged to watch you, David, hold Ben's paw as he stopped breathing. If any animal on earth gets to heaven, it would be Ben.

You will never have a better friend and companion. The days ahead without Ben will seem lonely, but you do have the one answer that many others don't—Jesus Christ, who this very week [2000 years ago] suffered unimaginably but conquered death and rose again in victory. God will grant you the grace and comfort and mercy to "help in time of need" (Hebrews 4:14–16).

David, Dad, and Mom, I know I can't alleviate your

suffering, but I will continue to support you with Christ's love in any way I can.

Love, Mark

I finished reading and continued to stare at the screen, trying to absorb the profound weight of Mark's words. The empathy. The perceptiveness. Mark got it. He got Ben. He got my relationship with Ben. He got the depths of sorrow we were experiencing. This from someone who hadn't spent much time with Ben aside from family gatherings and a few canoe trips. Mark had his own home and his own family. He had never even owned a dog. And yet he understood. Even more, on this Tuesday of Easter week, he directed us to the towering, transcendent perspective where comfort could be found.

I started writing my own email. After just four sentences, it seemed like enough. I was in a tenuous state, and more was not going to be better in this moment.

With "Ben" as the subject line, I pushed "send" on the following at 9:11 p.m. on Tuesday, April 3:

With great sorrow I tell you that my beloved Ben is gone. His condition suddenly worsened today and we decided to put him to sleep.

He was a precious gift from God and will never be forgotten. Thank you for your prayers and support during this trial.

David

At the end of the email, I attached a picture of Ben standing on top of a rock outcropping high above Lake Superior with the forest below splashed in peak fall color. I had taken the photo a few years back on one of our many hikes through the hills on the North Shore. It captured Ben well—athletic, handsome, good-natured . . . as one friend put it, "Majestic."

Yes, Ben had been all of that and more. But now he was gone and I was still here. The battle with cancer was over, but a new struggle with grief had immediately taken its place.

I went downstairs, crawled into bed, turned off the light, and lay there in the dark, feeling the painful sting of losing my beloved Ben. I dreaded that tomorrow would dawn and Ben wouldn't be there. My chest heaved uncontrollably as I wept on my bed.

Wearied from sorrow, I finally found sleep.

CHAPTER 15

A TIME TO MOURN
... A START TO HEAL

Sure enough, the next day dawned. It was early, much earlier than I normally wake up, but it didn't take a millisecond of consciousness for me to realize that Ben wasn't going to be next to my bed. I checked anyway, but all that I saw was an empty space of off-white carpet. It looked so horribly bare. There was no dog bed. There was no Ben looking up, waiting for me to invite him into bed.

It had been a fitful night of sleep that yielded little rejuvenation. I wanted to sleep more, just to escape, but that wasn't going to happen. I lay there for a while before the anguish forced me out of bed and upstairs to my parents' bedroom, where I found them awake early as well.

I was a grown man, a thirty-seven-year-old adult, who supported myself, lived on my own, had traveled the world, had seen plenty of life, even death, but all of that experience and self-sufficiency didn't make any difference right now. I lay down beside my parents in their bed, and for the next hour, we reminisced between tears about Ben—how great a dog he was, how much we missed him, and how our lives would never be the same.

Nothing had changed in the house—their bedroom was identical to yesterday, the couch in the living room was still positioned next to the window—but everything felt different. A discomfiting silence had come over the house, and it was palpable and painful.

Never again would we hear Ben's toenails clicking down the hallway on the hardwood floors as he walked back to my parents' bedroom to greet them in the morning. Never again would we hear his deep "Woof!" from the couch as he barked at someone on the lake. Never again would Ben be at our side to enhance every part of our day. The walks, the begging, the fetching, the swimming, the riding in the car. Never again.

That is what hurt about losing Ben—the *never*. It seemed that death had won and had stolen something of inestimable value to me.

It was a time to mourn. But little did I know that help and hope would be immediately offered. In fact, this time to mourn would be a vital first step on the road to heal.

* * *

True to form, life was there beckoning me to jump back in the morning after Ben died. Mark and I were scheduled to attend a noon luncheon to hear football coach Tony Dungy speak. We had made the plans weeks before and, of course, the luncheon had to be today of all days. The last thing I wanted to do was go anywhere or see anyone, let alone talk to anyone. Mark called to ask what I wanted to do, and I told him to go ahead without me.

At first he didn't try to persuade me otherwise, but then he called back and suggested that it might be good for me to get out of the house for a couple hours. "Get some fresh air, get your mind off Ben for a little while," he urged. I really didn't want to go but my reserves were too low to resist, and so I reluctantly agreed.

Mark drove up my parents' driveway later in the morning and I slumped in the front seat of his car on the way to the event, stirring depressing thoughts and hardly saying a word. It was jarring to be out in the world for the first time since losing Ben. I wasn't expecting flags to be lowered to half-staff or people to line the road to pay their respects, but life-as-usual was more than I was ready to face right now.

Tony Dungy spoke about his background and football and how God had changed his life. I'm sure it was good and would have been helpful for me, but I was just too numb to absorb much of it. It was the middle of Easter Week, an apt time to gain perspective on suffering and death, but that wasn't sinking in either. I hadn't lost my faith in God or anything; it was just that the grief inside me was overwhelming all else. It hadn't been twenty-four hours since I lost Ben, and I'm sure I was still in a kind of shock.

Mark brought me back to my parents' house where I spent most of the afternoon lying on their couch, incapacitated by grief. And regret. The thought of Ben's body at the vet hospital in Chicago for an autopsy sickened me. I kicked myself over and over for putting him through the surgery. *Why didn't I just listen to my mother that night in Chicago and come straight home before the operation? Why couldn't I accept the fact that Ben was terminally ill and just keep him comfortable in his final weeks? What was I thinking?*

Both my brothers came over separately later in the day to see how my parents and I were doing. Mark prayed for us, that God would give us some comfort. John brought up a few of his favorite memories with Ben, such as walking the woods up north for grouse and the farmlands out west for pheasants. At first I thought being reminded of the good old days would make me feel worse since those times were over now. But it actually felt good to escape the discouraging confines of the last few months and reminisce about better days with Ben, even if it was for just a few minutes.

* * *

I woke up the next morning still swimming in sorrow. I could tell that I wasn't going to be getting over this anytime soon. Yet something inside told me that this was okay. I loved Ben deeply. He had been my treasured companion, a permanent fixture by my side for nearly nine years. Losing him was a major loss, and major loss causes major grief. Seeking quick closure seemed like a poor plan, even unrealistic.

I went upstairs and sat down on the couch to do as I had done the day before, which was mourn over Ben. There was nothing else that I had the strength or desire to do. The present had lost its flavor, the future its interest. The imagery from the well-known line in Psalm 23—"I walk through the valley of the shadow of death"—was never more poignant. I really was in a deep valley over which Ben's death was casting a dark shadow.

In the midst of my melancholy, I decided to read the Bible. I did so on this day not so much because I was some saint responding to grief by turning to God, but because I had a commitment to keep. Thirteen years earlier, when I was twenty-four years old, I had committed to reading the Bible every day, and I figured I'd better get it done sooner rather than later before I became too depressed to do anything.

Reading the Scriptures daily had led to a major U-turn in my life, and I perceived that continuing the pattern would help keep me on track. It certainly had. Even so, there were many days when I didn't feel like reading the Bible, and there were others when I felt too busy. Yet even on these days, something inside would invariably remind me to read it, even if for just five minutes before turning off the light. I was always glad I did.

I had grown up in a Bible-reading, church-going family and considered myself a "believer" from my youngest days. And yet as I went through my teenage, college, and young adult years, a contradiction emerged between what I professed and what I practiced. I may have known about God and faith, but actually living it out was another story.

This contradiction weighed heavily on me for several years in my early twenties. It got to the point that I became so conflicted within that I decided to stay home from a series of tennis tournaments one winter to be alone and take stock of the direction of my life. For the first time, I began to earnestly and consistently read the Bible. As I did so over the course of a month, two things became clear: I was disobeying God more than I realized and would be held accountable; and the only way I could become right with God was through His Son, Jesus Christ.

And so it was in my mid-twenties, in the middle of my tennis career, in the middle of that Minnesota winter, that I responded to Jesus' call to "repent and believe in the gospel." I cried out to God and told Him that I desired to go His way instead of my own, and that I needed His help to do so. I sincerely believed that Jesus' perfect life and sacrificial death satisfied God's justice and wrath for my sin, and I wanted to obey and follow Him for the rest of my life.

To my great encouragement, my life began to turn in a whole new direction. There were plenty of opportunities to give in and slide back to my former way, but every time those temptations came, I would be reminded of a passage from the Bible that redirected my heart to what God wanted me to do. I didn't become perfect or anything like that, but I had a new strength and resolve that was inspired by trusting in God's Word rather than in my own human reasoning and desires.

I tell you this extra detail on my faith background to convey that reading the Bible wasn't just some desperate thing I did in the days after losing Ben. Throughout the whole ordeal with Ben, even on the hardest days, I somehow had managed to crack open my Bible to read a few verses.

It may seem counterintuitive that I would have to compel my-self to read the Bible after all the positive ways it had impacted me over the years, but such is the destabilizing impact of trials that can easily turn the most steady person into a rudderless craft being tossed about on the high seas. I knew with my mind that I should read the Bible because therein was truth and comfort, but the grief of the moment put me in an emotional state where I felt like doing nothing but sitting and sorrowing.

That Thursday, I began reading Psalm 119. I'm not sure why I chose this chapter. It is, after all, the longest chapter in the Bible. I may have been reading through the Psalms at the time, or I may have specifically selected the chapter because almost every verse refers to the power of the Word of God. Whatever the reason, I got to verse 28 and my eyes stopped on the page.

My soul is weary with sorrow; strengthen me according
to your word. (Psalm 119:28 NIV)

I was struck by how the first six words so aptly described my present condition. My soul was weary with sorrow. That weariness may have helped me fall asleep the night Ben died, but other than that, I don't even know how I was able to keep going after all that had taken place over the previous three months.

And yet there was a semicolon in the verse, as in, there is more to come. The second phrase didn't say, "Therefore, life is over—the end." No, the next six words declared that help is available: "strengthen me according to your word."

When we're weary, we need strength. When we're sorrowful, we need hope. This was me, exactly me. I was weary with sorrow and needed strength based on real hope, not a pull-myself-up-by-the-bootstraps finite strength based on a tomorrow-is-bound-to-be-better wishful hope.

No, the help for my soul that was weary with sorrow would be a potent strength far above and beyond what I could muster, and it would be based on the never-failing promises of God. Right there on the page in front of me was the first tiny ray of hope that I could be helped through this grief. "Strengthen me according to your word." That was what I needed.

Reading this verse was not some kind of magic bullet or the power of positive thinking. I didn't jump off the couch with a smile on my face and a spring in my step. Things didn't suddenly become "all better now." But this was an early promise that pointed the right way forward.

I knew it would take participation on my part. Putting the Bible under my pillow at night wasn't going to cut it. Inasmuch as I had lost my appetite for doing almost everything, I was going to have to feed myself with God's Word every day to be strengthened. I didn't know what the road ahead would be like, but I knew that if I read and trusted in the promises of God with all that I had, I would end up in a much better place than I was experiencing at that moment.

* * *

That evening, our church had its annual Maundy Thursday service. This was always the most somber gathering of the year, a time to remember Christ's last supper with his disciples before He was betrayed, arrested, and crucified the following morning. Talk about a service to match my mood.

Walking into the church, I felt that same disconnect between my internal sorrow and the walking, talking world around me. A few rows over from us, Brodie sat with her family. This was the first time I had seen her since Ben had died, and I could see in her eyes that she was peering into my soul to see how I was doing. By the expression on her face, I could tell I didn't look good.

The last two months, and especially the last month with Ben going downhill, had put our relationship on hold. We had gotten together occasionally for dinner—with Ben tagging along in his usual role of chaperone—but as Ben's condition worsened, my attention had turned fully to him. And now that I had lost him, I had withdrawn even more. Brodie was the type to understand, but my drifting away during my darkest trial revealed something amiss in our relationship that I'm sure she felt.

The pastor gave a short and serious message about Jesus' final night before His crucifixion, and then served communion. Listening to him describe how Jesus, the sinless Son of God, willingly gave up His life to be the sacrifice for our sins so that God's wrath and justice could be satisfied and we could be reconciled to God was powerful to contemplate.

I arrived back at my parents' house thinking about all that had happened that day: first, waking up and feeling the way I did and coming across that verse in Psalm 119 . . . and then this evening's service at church. I was too awash in grief to put it all together; but I had a sense, however faint, that important truth was being offered to me.

* * *

The next day was Good Friday, and after going back to church for a short noontime service, I drove to my own house for the first time since Ben had died. Everything felt so strange and empty and quiet without Ben. He was nowhere, but he was everywhere. His dog bed was still next to my bed, his food and dishes and toys were scattered about the porch, some of his medications were on the kitchen counter. And all the pictures of him and me were on the walls, the bed stand . . . everywhere. I didn't descend to the bottom of the valley again, but I sure felt as if I were heading that way.

After a few minutes of wandering and pondering, I went over to the desk in my bedroom. This was where I had spent most of my days typing away on my computer while Ben patiently slept beside me. It had been three days since losing Ben, and in that time, I had received upwards of fifty emails from friends and others expressing their sympathies over my loss. Some had written thoughtful, substantial notes; others just a sentence or two. Either way, I appreciated all of them, and it made me realize how helpful a word of kindness and support can be when a person is down.

So the last thing I was expecting — or prepared for — was an email that, in effect, challenged me for loving Ben and grieving over his loss. That someone who didn't even know me would write such a note, let alone so soon after Ben's death, pretty much defines presumption and insensitivity.

169

Apparently this person was a listener of my radio program who had written to me, as he put it, "to spare you from unnecessary heartache over animals ever again." As you read a few excerpts, you'll see that he didn't spare me anything at all.

David,

. . . When it comes time to say good-bye to a pet we should try to remember that we tend to put too much affection on animals because they are easy to "love." And the reason we are so upset is that we have made this pet into something it is not: a human. . . .

I recommend that Christians make a point not to anthropomorphize their pets. To do so, to set your affections on an animal instead of people, takes away from people those affections which should normally be for humans alone; we are wasting our emotions on animals, we are not guarding our hearts from unnatural affections. . . .

You must not steal from the people around you the tenderness you may be wasting on animals.

So remember, David, as you say goodbye to your dog, that he was only an animal. Jesus gave Himself away to people, not to animals.

I was practically shaking after reading this. We can be hurt and angry at the same time, but usually one will manifest itself more strongly than the other. Congratulations to this person, that he was able to elicit both out of me equally and simultaneously.

Of course, I shouldn't have been hurt or angry. Why should I have cared about the opinion of someone I didn't even know? Yet he was challenging the very nature of my relationship with Ben—as if I had been living for the last eight-and-a-half years in a way that displeased God.

As a Christian, I couldn't help but take this veiled criticism seriously. I may have resented the tone and timing of the email, but it forced me to examine myself to see if my love for Ben and all the grief I was feeling over losing him was in fact "unnatural affection."

The tricky part about receiving reproof like this is discerning the truth and eliminating the error. Yes, it was true that Jesus had come to earth to give His life for people, not animals. Animals don't have our "sin problem." They may do things we consider sin—steal from each other, even kill each other—but nowhere does the Bible say that God holds them accountable because they were not given and do not know the laws of God.

What touched a nerve, however, was the charge that my love and grief for Ben was somehow "stealing tenderness" from the people around me.

The truth is that Ben actually *added* to my human relationships rather than taking away from them. Family and friends loved that I brought Ben when we got together. They weren't thinking, *Boy, David's love for that dog takes away from his love for me*. In fact, I made many new friends because I did things that I would never have done and went places that I would never have gone if I hadn't had Ben.

It took some time, but I finally got past the email when I considered how Jesus might handle someone mourning the loss of a dog. I couldn't imagine Him saying, "Hey, don't sweat it; it was just a dog; don't waste your tenderness on an animal."

To the contrary, I think Jesus would put His arm around the person in compassion and weep with them over the effect of sin on the world, most graphically portrayed through death. And then He would offer hope. At least that's what Jesus did with those mourning the loss of His friend Lazarus (Luke 11).

* * *

I started getting ready for bed on that Friday evening with a lot on my mind. Death, more than any other experience in life, has an almost irresistible leverage to shift our focus from the temporal to the eternal. Here I had been cruising along in life, "doing my thing" as they say, working, traveling, enjoying time with family, friends, and Ben, when, out of the blue, disease knocked at my door, and then seven weeks later, death barged right in. It was like I had been transferred, against my will, from a house of peace into a house of mourning.

Hard questions about God, His purposes, disease and death were occupying my thoughts. I had just seen first-hand cancer take down Ben's body. Never had it been so poignant what the Bible says about our fallen world.

> Therefore, just as through one man sin entered into the world, and death through sin, and so death spread to all men, because all sinned. (Romans 5:12)

The corrupting effect of sin destroyed what had been beautiful to me. I hated it. I understood that I had contributed to it. And I knew that God was grieved over it because a world groaning from the consequences of sin was never His desire.

The grief over Ben, now three days after his death, was still weighing heavy on me. The email that I received earlier in the day had me thinking about things I really didn't want to consider at this time. And Easter, with all the talk of sin, suffering, and death—overcome by Christ's resurrection—pointed to something powerful for me to understand and apply. This was a lot for anyone to process, especially under distress.

As if on cue, another condolence email from an older friend of mine in California came in just as I was about to turn out the light. It was short and to the point.

Hi David,

So sorry to hear about your loss.

Here's a quote from an unidentified source: "It's Friday . . . but Sunday's coming!"

Have a blessed Resurrection Sunday!

Russ

The note seemed so brief as to negate any potential for significance. Only one sentence about Ben. Well, I guess one sentence of sympathy is better than paragraphs telling me that I shouldn't have loved him so much.

I read over the second line again. *"It's Friday . . . but Sunday's coming!"* This wasn't a direct quote from the Bible, but it was obvious what he meant. Today was the terrible day that Christ was crucified, but Sunday is coming, when Christ rose victorious over the grave.

Russ was trying to cheer me up. "Today is your bad day, David, but there will be better days ahead," is how I superficially interpreted his words. That sounded nice and it was appreciated, but I certainly didn't feel a whole lot of hope for the days ahead.

What I didn't fully grasp, however, was that there was something far more profound in Russ's words than simply, "Cheer up, things will get better." Jesus' death and resurrection wasn't just some feel-good message or religious tradition to be observed every Easter; rather, there was something very personal and powerful in it that would be the basis for the comfort, strength, and perspective I so desperately needed after losing Ben.

As I put my head on the pillow that night still grieving over Ben, I didn't realize that I had just been shown another ray of hope . . . actually, the ultimate foundation for hope.

CHAPTER 16

FOUNDATION FOR HOPE

Everything became a "first" after losing Ben. Friday was the first time I returned to my house without Ben. Friday night was the first time I slept in my own room without him. Firsts cropped up everywhere because, well, Ben had always been with me everywhere.

One of the worst firsts was going for a walk without Ben. It hurt the first time, the second time, the twentieth time. Rain or shine, sleet or snow, getting outside every day for a walk had been our daily ritual his entire life. To all of a sudden be out walking solo seemed just that—*so lonely.*

There is something ethereal about the simple act of walking a dog, something that has refreshed body and soul for as long as man and dog have been together. Of course there's the companion aspect to it. But it's more than that. It's the enhancement, the entertainment, if you will, that Ben provided along the way. Just seeing him all happy and athletic, trotting to and fro, greeting other dogs, fetching the retrieving dummy, taking a swim at the beach, and chasing after squirrels was something that I greatly missed. After the first few walks without him, I remember thinking, *Why am I doing this?*

I was in the same apathetic state of mind as I contemplated whether or not to host my radio show on the first Saturday after losing Ben. With the topic and guest scheduled well in advance, I figured it was easier to formulate a few questions and let the guest talk for most of the hour than it was to cancel everything and find an old show to air. So there I was, driving to the studio to interview a scientist on "The Evidence and Meaning of Easter" without Ben in his usual spot in the front passenger seat.

I already knew that I wanted to devote a whole program at some point to dealing with the loss of a pet . . . but not on this Saturday. I did, however, spend a few minutes in the opening segment telling listeners that I had put Ben down on Tuesday and that I was grieving because he had been like a son to me.

In using the "losing a dog is like losing a child" analogy, I knew some wouldn't get it ("You think a dog is equal to a child?") or wouldn't like it ("How dare you compare losing your dog to losing a child!"). For better or for worse though, we dog lovers make this dogs-are-like-kids analogy to try to help people understand how meaningful our dogs are to us. We think it will help them grasp why we are so crushed when losing him or her.

Is losing a dog like losing a child? I guess for the literal answer you would have to ask someone who has loved and lost both a child and a dog. But a literal comparison is not the point. The point is that losing a dog can be *like* losing a child, as in, perhaps not the same degree of grief, but a *similar* kind of grief. If someone you're trying to explain this to doesn't get this nuance after a couple attempts, I suggest you change the subject.

And that's what I did on the radio program. After three or four minutes on Ben, I moved away from my personal trial to the advertised topic of the day, "The Evidence and Meaning of Easter." What I did not anticipate was how much context this topic would provide for what I was going through at the time.

I set up the interview by saying something to the effect that after two thousand years and as many traditions and interpretations later, it is often concluded that the Easter story is just that—a story. Or perhaps a legend, a fable, a myth.

My guest on the program that day did not hold that view. Dr. Don Bierle was a PhD with advanced degrees, a published scientist, college professor, and a former skeptic when it came to matters of faith. But after meticulously researching the Bible to see if there was factual validity to its claims, especially with regard to the life, death, and resurrection of Jesus, Dr. Bierle had come to the conclusion that the Bible is true and Jesus is who He said He was.

Dr. Bierle had gone from agnostic to believer, and since then, his mission in life had become "to proclaim the gospel with evidence," as he put it.

The doctor certainly knew his stuff and provided plenty of evidence for his conclusions. Among other things, he showed—even using non-biblical sources—that Jesus was, in fact, a real person who lived at the time the Bible says He did ("as real a historical figure as George Washington"). He pointed out that the date when Jesus rode a donkey into Jerusalem to present Himself to the Jewish nation, known as the "triumphal entry" on Palm Sunday, had been predicted 483 years earlier in the Old Testament book of Daniel.

What's more, Dr. Bierle said that the eyewitness accounts of the men and women who found Jesus' tomb empty, along with the over five hundred people who saw Jesus alive after His death, would lead any reasonable person to conclude that Jesus did, in fact, rise from the dead.

Being a Christian, it didn't take much convincing for me to

agree with his points. In fact, after hearing all this, I came to the conclusion that it would take more faith to *not* believe it.

I then asked the doctor a follow-up question, "With so much concrete evidence, why do people still not believe in Jesus?"

Granted, this is a hard question for a scientist—or anyone—to answer. It moves the conversation from the *what* to the *why*. But that, after all, was the second part of the topic of the day—"The Evidence [the what] and the Meaning [the why] of Easter."

Dr. Bierle sort of chuckled as if to say, "Well, that is the $64,000 question." And then he went on to offer several possible explanations. Some people may simply not know the evidence about Jesus. Others may know it but don't believe it; and still others may know and even intellectually believe the evidence, yet aren't willing to have Jesus reign in their lives.

He pointed out that Jesus' works and words don't leave any middle ground when it comes to our response to Him. The miraculous things He did—like healing people with diseases, raising the dead, turning water into wine, calming storms, and walking on water—coupled with the outrageous claims He made about Himself such as, "I and the Father are one," or "I am the way, and the truth, and the life; no one comes to the Father but through Me," left only two possible conclusions about His identity. Either Jesus was the biggest liar and fraud of all time, or He was who He claimed to be—the Son of God in human flesh and the only One who can reconcile sinful man to Holy God.

I was tracking closely with what Dr. Bierle was saying because I had experienced this tension in my own life. I had believed for as long as I could remember that Jesus is a real person, that He performed miracles, that He is the Son of God, and that He died and rose from the dead. But for some reason, that belief didn't significantly alter the way I chose to live my life.

As I mentioned earlier, in my mid-twenties, when I finally saw myself for who I really was—a sinner in need of saving—I repented and put my trust in Jesus Christ as my Savior and Lord. It was then that my faith descended from my head down into my heart, and once there, pumped through and permeated every part of my being. It was only then that my mind, my will, and my desires started working together in obedience to God. This was not a check-your-brain-at-the-door blind faith. This was a conscious, rational decision that I made to step down from the throne of my life and turn the kingship over to Christ in order to follow Him.

Every aspect of my life was impacted. But that doesn't mean I was exempt from experiencing the same trials and feeling the same pains that come with living in this fallen world. As I drove home from the radio studio that Saturday morning—for the first time without Ben—I still carried a great weight of grief. Being a follower of Jesus didn't magically vaporize that. But the good news was the foundation that had been formed and fortified in the years since giving my life over to Christ was starting to provide stability in this storm and would become my basis for comfort and hope going forward.

Just days after losing Ben, I began to understand the bigger picture. A sin-stricken world with its terminal consequences was ultimately the reason Ben had died, but sin was also the reason that Jesus Christ had come to earth. He lived in our fallen realm. He saw the effects of sin. He even experienced death. But unlike anyone else, Jesus had complete victory over sin and death and promised the same to those who would believe in Him. The apostle Paul explained,

For since by a man [Adam] came death, by a man [Jesus

Christ] also came the resurrection of the dead. . . . But when this perishable will have put on the imperishable, and this mortal will have put on immortality, then will come about the saying that is written, "Death is swallowed up in victory. O death, where is your victory? O death, where is your sting?" The sting of death is sin, and the power of sin is the law; but thanks be to God, who gives us the victory through our Lord Jesus Christ. (1 Corinthians 15:21, 54–57)

I had read this well-known passage before. But now that I had seen and felt the sting of death up close and personal, I started to think deeply about what it meant. How exactly does Jesus give victory over sin and death when both are everywhere and inevitable in our world?

I found the answer in the last chapters of the Bible, where Jesus says that in the future, He will destroy this corrupted world and create a "new heaven and a new earth" where "there will no longer be any death; there will no longer be any mourning, or crying, or pain." And He promises that those who believe in Him will join Him there to live with Him forever.

Then I saw a new heaven and a new earth; for the first heaven and the first earth passed away, and there is no longer any sea. And I saw the holy city, new Jerusalem, coming down out of heaven from God, made ready as a bride adorned for her husband. And I heard a loud voice from the throne, saying, "Behold, the tabernacle of God is among men, and He will dwell among them, and they shall be His people, and God Himself will be among them, and He will wipe away every tear from their eyes; and there will no longer be any death; there will no longer be any mourning, or crying, or pain; the first things have passed away."

And He who sits on the throne said, "Behold, I am making all things new." And He said, "Write, for these words are faithful and true." Then He said to me, "It is done. I am the Alpha and the Omega, the beginning and the end. I will give to the one who thirsts from the spring of the water of life without cost. He who overcomes will inherit these things, and I will be his God and he will be My son. But for the cowardly and unbelieving and abominable and murderers and immoral persons and sorcerers and idolaters and all liars, their part will be in the lake that burns with fire and brimstone, which is the second death." (Revelation 21:1–8)

This was both encouraging and sobering. It was incredibly encouraging to know that those who believe in Jesus Christ in this life can live with the expectant hope that when they depart this world, they will be ushered into a perfect eternal home where God will dwell with them, and where there will be no more sin and death. But as I read the last sentence, it was sobering to consider that unbelievers will spend eternity suffering in an unspeakably horrible place.

I thought about Russ's email. "It's Friday . . . but Sunday's coming!" Friday was about sin and death in our fallen world. I had just seen firsthand what that looked like, and it was ugly. But Sunday is coming with victory and hope for a new heaven and new earth, where all will be made right by God.

I went to church the following morning on Easter Sunday.

All around me worshippers were celebrating Jesus' resurrection. The message was loud and clear: sin and death were overcome by Jesus Christ; Jesus is who He said He was—the Son of God and Savior of mankind. Who else could have paid for the sins of mankind? Who else has power over death? Who else could fulfill this promise?

> I am the resurrection and the life; he who believes in Me will live even if he dies, and everyone who lives and believes in Me will never die. (John 11:25–26)

There it was—the believer's ultimate foundation for hope. A hope that I knew about, but had not been setting my whole heart on. The deep grief of losing Ben had distracted and destabilized me. It was like I had been floating in an ocean without a map and rudder to guide me back into the safety of port. Contrary winds were blowing me toward desolate islands of depression and bitterness. Thank God I was being offered a lifeline.

In these early days after Ben's death, when I was shaken to the core, I was fortunate that words of truth that pointed the way to real hope and comfort were presented to my wounded soul. Wrong "ointments" could have been applied to my wound only to make things worse. I do not pat myself on the back for "making the right calls." Rather, it seemed in my darkest moments, at times of crushing grief and lacking hope, even when God seemed far away, that the right remedy was being offered that would set a good healing process in motion.

That it was Easter week when Ben died only made the lesson easier to grasp. Having my thoughts directed away from my own painful circumstances—even for short spurts—and toward the immensely greater suffering of Jesus Christ and what His life and

death meant for me and all of mankind, was the best perspective I could have possibly been given.

This didn't mean my grief would be gone by the next day or even the next week. Deep wounds don't go away like that. A glimmer of hope doesn't immediately erase grief. But hope based on real truth does start and perpetuate good healing. It was a healing *process* that I would have to go through, not a healing *moment*. In the end, there would be a scar, as there is with every deep wound, but it would serve as a reminder that healing doesn't mean "back to normal," but rather a "new normal" and stronger for the trial.

CHAPTER 17

NOT OVER, BUT THROUGH

Monday came and it felt strange. My first week back to work without Ben. I looked at my calendar and over the following two weeks there were things to do, people to meet, places to go. There was a dentist appointment, a guest-hosting stint for another radio show, a meeting with an accountant, a garage-door project, a board meeting, and all the usual work in between.

My regular life had been put on the back burner for the previous few months; but it had been six days since losing Ben and a new week was here, ready or not. Forgetting the past would not be possible, but forging ahead would still be required. How was I ever going to do that? I didn't have the strength or desire to "get back in the game," and that was an unsettling place to be.

Paramount now would be to trust in and hang on to the foundation for hope that I had been hearing over the last several days. That was easier said than done. As we all know, hearing something or knowing something doesn't necessarily equate to believing it and putting it into practice. Rather, each day when the grief and inevitable reminders of Ben would surface, I would need to consciously and deliberately reach for these promises and hold onto them with everything I had.

It is in this weakened, dependent state that God would work powerfully if I was willing. The apostle Paul stated, "I will rather boast about my weaknesses, so that the power of Christ may dwell in me . . . for when I am weak, then I am strong" (2 Corinthians 12:9–10). Paul had learned that real strength to overcome life's trials was not found in his own self-sufficiency, but rather in God's all-sufficient resources from above.

That God often uses regular people to point us to things above became apparent later in the day. Having entered that dead zone where the initial shock and raw emotion of losing Ben had receded to leave an emptiness in their place, I went to my mailbox to find a letter from a woman named Jeanne whom I didn't know. Through the radio show she heard that I had lost Ben, and she had taken it upon herself to handwrite me a note. This would be a far different message from the one I had received a few days earlier about loving animals more than loving people. Jeanne's letter was like fresh air for my soul, full of sympathy, encouragement, and hope.

Dear David,

How sorry I am to hear of your great loss this week — Ben, beloved and faithful family companion. My sure hope and prayer for you and your family is that the "God of all comfort" will be abundantly apparent and sufficient through your grief.

"Blessed be the God and Father of our Lord Jesus Christ, the Father of mercies and God of all comfort, who comforts us in all our affliction so that we will be able to comfort those who are in any affliction with the comfort with which we ourselves are comforted by God. . . . For as many as are the promises of God, in Him they are yes." (2 Corinthians 1:3–4, 20)

About one-and-a-half years ago, I had to put my special friend Sparky to sleep. He went very quickly downhill over a period of three weeks due to a tumor in his nasal cavity. What difficulty it was to try to comfort and care for him, and he kept getting worse! But God showed His faithfulness to me during that time in a way I had not experienced before: words from His Word that jumped off the page to give comfort and hope, cards from friends, a pastor's sermon. God has all at His command to accomplish His good purposes—even in the comfort of one of His own who is experiencing great loss.

And maybe our pets will be in heaven. (Does Isaiah 11:6–9 describe the new heaven and new earth?)

May your sadness and sorrow make your heart even more tender to the majesty and love of our Lord Jesus Christ, and may His joy be your strength.

Jeanne

I finished the letter, trying to soak in all that Jeanne had said in a few short paragraphs. The expression of empathy and kindness. The pointing to the promises and purposes of God in the midst of trials. The reference to God as the "Father of compassion and the God of all comfort." Even the possibility of pets in heaven based on Isaiah's prophecy of the time when "the lion will lie down with the lamb." Talk about building someone up with a foundation for hope.

Throughout this trial with Ben, I, like most people when encountering death, grappled with the "Why is God allowing this to happen?" question. I mean, God is God—He could have kept this from happening if He had wanted to, right?

I understood the macro answer to the question. We live in a fallen world and death happens to everyone and everything. But trying to figure out the personal answer, as in, *Why Ben, why me, why now?* seemed like something I could never really know.

The response-bordering-on-cliché I'd often heard was, "God has a higher plan!" This didn't feel very satisfying though, especially when it was tossed out by someone who hadn't experienced a trial similar to mine. My natural response was not to break out in praise of God's higher plan in the midst of my lowest moments. Praising while paining didn't seem to go together, but alas, there it was in the passage that Jeanne quoted in her letter, "Praise be to the God and Father of our Lord Jesus Christ, the Father of compassion and the God of all comfort."

I found this "praise God" response to trials all the more remarkable, considering the apostle Paul was the one saying it. This was a man who wasn't theorizing about trials, but rather one who had experienced them full force. He was beaten, persecuted, imprisoned, and eventually martyred for preaching about Christ, and yet here he was, still praising God for His compassion and comfort. He obviously understood something I didn't.

There was something else that Jeanne brought up that I had been struggling with. Where is Ben now? If I knew for certain that Ben had gone to heaven and that I would join him there someday, that would have been a wonderfully encouraging word.

But I wasn't so sure. I knew what I hoped, I knew what most

dog lovers would say, I knew how pets-in-heaven books end, but a clear biblical basis for concluding that Ben is in heaven seemed sketchy at best. I searched long and hard in the Bible. I researched the views of scholars I respected and either little was said or divergent conclusions were made. There was no consensus.

Of course I knew very well what the Bible says about the afterlife for humans. Jesus said plainly, "He who believes in the Son has eternal life; but he who does not obey the Son will not see life, but the wrath of God abides on him" (John 3:36).

But what about animals? What happens after they die? Do they just return "dust to dust," forever annihilated from existence? Or does God give them new, resurrected bodies, as He does human believers, to spend eternity with Him in heaven? If so, does this mean all animals, even spiders and snakes, go to heaven . . . or just pets?

These are hard questions. Scripture doesn't give the kind of "animals will either go here or there" clarity as it does about the eternal destiny of humans. So I had to nibble around the edges of passages that describe heaven and then try to draw conclusions that are consistent with the character of God. I may have had real assurance and hope that I was going to heaven after I died, but I couldn't say the same about Ben and that made me feel uneasy.

Many more weeks would go by before I began to gain a better understanding about whether I would see Ben again someday and what God's higher purpose was for me in this trial. Yet the way Jeanne presented these two issues had encouraged me. To her, it wasn't a question of whether God was comforting and compassionate and praiseworthy in the midst of trials or whether He had a higher purpose in it for me. He was and He did. And even though she wasn't so certain about pets in heaven, she suggested it might be so. Jeanne had given me a word from above just when I needed it.

* * *

It was almost three weeks after losing Ben, and I had yet to get together with Brodie. It's not that it was inconvenient to see her—her house was only blocks away from my parents'. The truth was that I didn't have the desire to get together. The trial with Ben and the grief that followed had drained my interest in dating.

Or perhaps it revealed that there was something missing in our relationship.

This was disheartening because Brodie and I always seemed to have a solid foundation for a good marriage. We had a lifelong friendship, shared faith, and many common interests. She even had a black Lab. Surely love, marriage, and a baby carriage were in our future.

At least, that is what I had in mind when we had begun dating again five years after breaking up. This time around though, neither of us could have anticipated that a months-long ordeal with Ben would have the effect of bringing our relationship to a halt.

But it had. My trial with Ben had not drawn me closer to Brodie—a bad sign, considering our next step most likely would have been engagement. Instead, when the going got tough, I backed away as if this were my own personal trial and "no one could possibly understand what I am going through." When I honestly examined myself though, I could see that my behavior over the past month had revealed that something was lacking. I didn't have a strong desire to be married, and my retreat from the relationship after losing Ben showed me that. I needed to stop wasting Brodie's time.

Rain was pouring down as I walked up to Brodie's house that Sunday night. I knew what I had to say. I knew it would hurt her. And while I figured she knew something was amiss over the last month, she surely didn't see this coming.

I explained to her what I just explained to you, and while it's good to tell the truth, the truth can sometimes hurt. It did. This was the second time we had dated, and in her mind, it was time to give up on this dream and move on. I drove home on a dark, wet night trying to get a hold on how I had lost my dog and likely a wife in the span of three weeks.

* * *

The calendar turned to May and the post-grief grief started to set in. No one can agonize forever after losing a loved one. Those first days and weeks of raw grief are so taxing that body and soul eventually become drained of their emotional fuel. When the initial storm finally subsides (with *when* being of unspecified duration depending on the person), a different kind of grief moves in like a heavy fog graying out the landscape and refusing to lift.

Those unbearably sharp pangs that I had felt for weeks after Ben's death gave way to a dull ache, serving as a constant reminder that something was not right.

Of course, what was not right was that Ben was not around. I labored through May trying to carry on with my usual responsibilities, all the while feeling as if I were just going through the motions. I don't know how I looked, but I felt blank. Several times a day, in the middle of thinking about this or that, or moving from here to there, I found myself stopped in my tracks, bewildered and shaking my head over Ben being gone.

By this point, I was an experienced single. I knew what it was like to be and live alone. But being alone is different from being lonely, and I began to feel the latter despite the fact that my family and friends were nearby. They and others had expressed their kind sympathies and written cards of encouragement and support, and I appreciated that. But that was last month, and I couldn't expect them to keep propping me up. They had lives and families of their own and they needed to carry on. So did I. And that was the hard part.

If grief could be graphed, it would be nice to think that there would be a line that started at my lowest point—say, the day I lost Ben—and then ascended in a perfectly straight forty-five-degree angle upward until I reached full normalization of life.

Unfortunately, we don't live in a world like that. We live in a fallen world where emotions wax and wane, circumstances change, and setbacks occur. I'd always heard that time heals, and I would have thought that five weeks, six weeks, and now seven weeks after losing Ben, I would have bounced back to something resembling my normal self. But I hadn't. I felt like a shell of myself, all hollow on the inside. The grief had changed, but this new post-grief grief didn't taste very good either, and I wondered if or when I'd ever get over this.

That was my problem. I had been trying to "get over this." What I didn't realize is that God was bringing me *through* this. I wanted this trial to be *over*—the sooner the better—because the pain hurt so much. But I was going to have to learn that *through* accepts the trial, knowing that restoration and growth are taking place along the way.

I may have been doing the right things: reading Scripture, trusting as best I could in God's promises, and praying for strength and comfort. I had the right foundation for hope, but my desire and expectation was that doing these things would be the means of getting over the trial. *All right, I've checked the right boxes— can I get over this now?*

God, on the other hand, had another plan. He was not letting this trial go to waste. His top priority was not to relieve me of the pain but rather to forge my good and display His glory through it. And He wasn't going to bring me through it before His purposes had been accomplished. At the same time, He wasn't going to let me be crushed and ruined under the weight of the trial either.

God had me right where He wanted and that was in the palm of His hand. I just needed to rest there and receive His healing in His time.

* * *

I didn't get all this as the month of May came to a close, but something my mother had shared with me a week after Ben died was beginning to take root. She had been reading through the New Testament letter written by the apostle Peter to fellow Christians who were suffering persecution. No doubt my mom was reading Peter's letter to glean something that she could apply to her own anguish over losing Ben.

Peter exhorted these persecuted Christians to rejoice because their willingness to endure hardship proved their faith was genuine and that they would receive eternal reward for suffering like their Savior and Lord.

Peter closed his letter with these words, which my mom had written on a half-sheet of notebook paper and given to me soon after losing Ben:

May the God of all grace, who called us to His eternal

glory by Christ Jesus, after you have suffered a while, perfect, establish, strengthen, and settle you. To Him be the glory and the dominion forever and ever. Amen. (1 Peter 5:10–11 NKJV)

These two verses were speaking to me as they had to my mother. I kept the scrap of paper and read it almost every day. It became my go-to passage, a summary of everything I was experiencing. I had "suffered a while"; I was trying my best to trust that God would "perfect, establish, strengthen, and settle" me through this. If Jesus' victory over sin and death was my foundation for hope, then this passage explained God's building plan once that foundation was laid.

These verses corresponded with what Jeanne had quoted from the apostle Paul in her note to me—that God is to be praised even for the hard things because He is in control, that He has a plan for my good and His glory, and that He will help me through it as "the God of all comfort."

It was curious to me that Paul referred to God as "the God of all comfort," while Peter called Him "the God of all grace." What was the difference? Did it matter?

I thought back over the two months since Ben had died. All I wanted was "the God of all comfort." I had lost something dear to me and I was hurting badly. I needed God's comfort, and He had been giving me just enough to buoy me above the turbulent waters of grief. Any less, and I would have descended beneath the surface into depression. Any more, and I would have gotten "over it" instead of being brought "through it."

But "the God of all grace"? What exactly did that mean? It sounded like one of those can't-quite-put-your-finger-on-it concepts.

I looked at the paper on which my mother had written that passage. I had it basically memorized by now. "May the God of all grace, who called us to His eternal glory by Christ Jesus, after you have suffered a while, perfect, establish, strengthen, and settle you."

The God of all grace. Whatever that meant, however it operated, God's grace seemed like something I needed right now.

And boy, was He about to give it.

CHAPTER 18

"JUST TO LOOK"

"The best thing you can do is get a new puppy ASAP. Do you want the name of my breeder?"

Seventeen minutes. That was how long it took for one of my friends to offer this suggestion after receiving my email regarding Ben's passing. It was the first response I received, and I'm sure it was well-intentioned and all. But as for my heeding his advice? Uh, no.

In fact, I don't even remember contemplating getting another dog during the entire time Ben was failing. The mere thought would have made me feel like I was betraying my best friend during his time of greatest need. Even after Ben died, I could hardly bear the thought of getting another dog. I had invested so much into Ben that starting over and pouring myself into a new puppy seemed like a mountain that I had little desire to climb.

Besides, how would any new dog ever live up to Ben? With an unattainable standard, wouldn't I forever be disappointed? And then to have to watch another one die? I'm sorry, but once in a lifetime of what I had just experienced was more than enough for me.

And yet something inside me kept pushing back against these

"never again" feelings. I loved dogs, we always had dogs, and with Ben, my level of dog-owning had risen to a whole new level. Was I really going to let these last months of agony overshadow and outweigh the eight-plus years of joy I had with Ben, and never get another dog simply because of the bitter end? Wasn't it better to have loved and lost Ben than never to have loved him at all? Deep down, I knew the answer to that question.

And so in my mind, the door was cracked slightly open. But I was in no mood to open it more fully and walk through anytime soon. I figured if I ever did get another puppy that it would be a minimum of six months to a year down the road, maybe more. I knew that it was going to take time, and lots of it, to heal before I could muster the courage to restart the dog lover's journey that inevitably goes from deep love to devastating loss. At this point, I wasn't even close to wanting any part of that.

But I decided to write some things down just in case. If or when the time did come to get another puppy, the specific aspects that I appreciated about Ben—the finer details of his character and conformation—could be lost to my fading memory. Pictures and videos weren't going to be enough. I needed to describe Ben on paper while he was still fresh in my mind.

And so in mid-May, I drafted an email to Donna Reece, the breeder who introduced us to Ben many summers ago. Included was a detailed description of Ben so that she would know what kind of puppy I was looking for should that day ever come.

I didn't send the email right away. I figured that I would think of more things to add later, and so I decided to let the note sit for a while. After all, the earliest I would even consider getting a new puppy would be many months down the road.

* * *

The first day of June arrived, and that meant summer had officially begun in Minnesota. Here, summer is strictly defined as June, July, and August—three months and not one day more. Sure, we may feel something resembling summer in May or September, but we don't let that fool us. May will always be the tail of spring and September the head of fall. Folks in these parts may complain about the weather, but they are proud of their four seasons. (And all Minnesotans said, "Amen.")

This June debuted on a Friday, which meant that I would be spending the greater part of the day preparing for my radio program that would take place the next morning. This particular Saturday—June 2—also happened to mark the day I turned thirty-eight.

Not that I was in any mood to celebrate. It was going to be yet another day of adjusting to life without Ben. He wouldn't be there as he always had been for my radio show. He wouldn't be there sleeping courtside, as he always had, for a tennis clinic I was to host later in the morning. And he wouldn't be there as he always had been, in the midst of us, as one of us, for a birthday dinner at my brother's house.

Sunday wasn't looking much better. That would be June 3, the two-month anniversary of Ben's death. How could it have been two months already? It seemed like that horrible day occurred just yesterday. And yet the long travail of grief over the last two months made it seem like ages ago.

Another weekend without Ben would be hard enough, but now it was the start of a whole new season without him. There would be no wading out in the lake with him on hot summer days to take a swim. There would be no open-air rides with him in the Jeep. There would be no casual walks through the neighborhood with the sun on our backs. I would be going through this summer alone without my boy.

And I didn't feel good about it. The cumulative effect of the whole ordeal had congealed into a kind of melancholy where I was carrying on but with little zest for life. Anyone who knew me well could see it in my eyes and face a mile away. It wasn't like me to be so bleak, so bland, so . . . blank. But that's what I had become. I may have had the right foundation for hope, but where was the rebound, the renewal? Where was the joy?

The phone rang at my house in the mid-morning on Friday. It was my mother. No surprise there—we talked on the phone almost every day. The conversation usually began with typical family matters related to what's up and what's next, but before long, my mother would invariably plunge the discussion to where she liked to go: deep and personal.

Rare would be the call where valuable nuggets of wisdom gained over her lifetime weren't imparted to me. This could mean a critique of something going on in the world or counsel for something going on in my life. Almost always, though, it entailed her conveying some profound spiritual truth that she had heard from one of the many sermons she listened to daily on her portable audio device. Serious and straightforward and never at a lack for depth and breadth—that's my mother.

This day, however, she called about something a little less didactic. The previous evening a friend of our family named Daniel had phoned her about two yellow Lab puppies he had seen stumbling around the sidelines at his daughter's soccer game. Daniel, a previous Lab owner who was looking for a new puppy, was compelled to walk over to the woman who had brought the puppies so he could find out more about the litter. The woman, named Sharon, was there to watch her daughter play soccer.

It also turned out that Sharon was a veterinarian.

Sharon told Daniel some background on the puppies, how she had bred her own female Lab with a male Lab from Wisconsin, and that six puppies had been born some seven weeks earlier. Four of the puppies were already settling into their new homes, and the two at the soccer field—one male and one female—were all that remained.

Daniel noticed the pups' blocky heads and big paws. They had that distinctive look of well-proportioned Labs bred for the show ring rather than the more wiry look common to Labs bred for hunting. The puppies were gorgeous from the tips of their noses to the tips of their tails.

Somehow the conversation circled back to the parents of the puppies, and Sharon offhandedly mentioned that the dogs came from a line called Ridge View Labradors.

"Ridge View Labradors?" Daniel repeated with surprise. "As in, Donna Reece?" He couldn't believe it.

Daniel knew all about Ridge View Labradors. He knew Ben was a Ridge View Lab. In fact, he had just looked into getting a puppy from Donna before finally deciding to put a down payment on a puppy from another breeder closer to home. A few years back, Donna had moved her kennel from a relatively close four-hour drive in Iowa to a new location fourteen hours away in the outskirts of Cleveland, Ohio, and that just seemed a bit too far to travel.

Daniel was amazed by the coincidence. What were the chances of coming across two Ridge View puppies at a soccer field five miles from his house in Minnesota when the actual kennel was eight hundred miles away in Ohio? And looking down at the two little ivory-colored bundles of fur in his lap, he started to wonder whether he had made the right decision on a puppy. It was plain to see that these pups were everything Ridge View dogs are known for: the beautiful look, the sweet face, the soft disposition.

Daniel sat there, torn. These were great puppies. But he was also expecting a great puppy from his breeder in Minnesota. And he would lose his down payment if he canceled. He went back and forth in his mind.

And then he called my parents.

I listened quietly as my mother relayed all this. To me, this was a nice story about a friend looking at some Lab puppies. But this was Daniel's story, not mine.

My mother didn't see it that way. There were *two* Ridge View puppies in the story, not just one. And they were right here in our backyard, just a short drive away. My mom was clearly interested . . . and not just for Daniel. She wanted to go see the puppies herself—and the sooner, the better.

I tried to temper her enthusiasm by explaining that the puppies may very well have Ridge View genes, but they weren't from the actual Ridge View kennel where Donna had carefully chosen a suitable male and female to breed based on characteristics that only she knew from years of breeding. And these pups hadn't been born and whelped in Donna's kennel with all the early socialization that she invests into each puppy. I didn't go so far as to call it a "backyard breeding" (in the negative sense of the term), but it probably crossed my mind.

My mom was not dissuaded. She wanted to see the puppies and she wanted me to go with her. "You and Dad go ahead," I replied. "I'm just not interested in getting a puppy right now, let alone one that isn't from Donna. I think we should stick with our plan."

I sat there for a moment after we hung up, staring into space and thinking about what I had just heard. *There are two seven-*

week-old Ridge View puppies available right now fifteen minutes from here? I asked myself rhetorically. I had to admit, that did seem pretty coincidental—almost weird.

But we wouldn't get pick of the litter, I quickly reminded myself, thinking back to how we got Ben. And if Daniel chose the male, all that would be left would be a female . . . and we definitely wanted another male like Ben. And the father of the puppies was back in Wisconsin, so we wouldn't be able to see him as we had both of Ben's parents. And we really didn't know much about the backgrounds of these puppies as we had with Ben. And we would be rushing into a major decision . . . and getting a dog *is* a major decision. And besides, I wasn't anywhere near ready for another dog.

Twenty reasons were ticked off in my head why we shouldn't get one of these puppies before I could come up with one why we should—and that had to do with their proximity. But what kind of reason is that for getting a puppy—because they're nearby? That sounded like something we'd do in our old days of dog ownership before we "came to the light" in getting Ben.

I rested the case in my mind and went back to work for the remainder of the day, hardly giving it another thought. I went to bed that night hardly giving it another thought. I woke up on my birthday the following morning hardly giving it another thought. I hosted my radio show hardly giving it another thought. I went to the tennis clinic later in the morning hardly giving it another thought.

And then my mother walked up to me after the tennis clinic and made me give it another thought.

My parents had come to watch me play a short exhibition match that was part of the event, and afterward, as I stood in the parking lot talking with them, my mother eventually got around to bringing up you-know-what. "Dad and I would like to go see the puppies today — would you like to come with us?"

What was I going to say? I didn't really have a good excuse not to go. It was early Saturday afternoon. My responsibilities were finished for the day. All that remained was a birthday dinner at my brother's house later that evening. The day was gorgeous, sunny, and temperate, one of those "rare days in June" that poet James Russell Lowell wrote about. It seemed like there were worse things to do than take a short drive with my parents to see a couple Lab puppies.

I looked at my mother. Standing before me was an extraordinary woman. And it had nothing to do with her physical stature. I, at six-feet-four inches, towered over her slight frame by almost a foot. Rather, it was her intellectual and spiritual acuity that set her apart from any woman I had ever met. Many times I have been told by others, "When I talk to your mother, I feel like she's looking right through me." The truth is, she is. Her piercing gaze is the external manifestation of the razor-sharp discernment behind it.

At this moment, though, as I looked down at her, something else was coming through those eyes beyond her usual gravity and sobriety. I could see anticipation and hope. My mom was clearly looking forward to seeing these puppies. Something inside her was leading her irresistibly to them. For the first time in months, after all the confusion, struggle, and sorrow over Ben, there was noticeable brightness in her eyes and face. She really wanted to do this.

This time I didn't turn her down. It's not that I wanted to go; it's that I knew I would be disappointing her if I didn't. She wanted me, her youngest son and the one with whom she had shared the life and trials of Ben, to go see these puppies with her.

My yielding went beyond a sense of obligation though. Her enthusiasm was communicating something to me. I realized that this was becoming more than a nice story about a friend of ours coming across two Lab puppies at a soccer game. My mom was thinking we might be a part of the story as well.

With a touch of reluctance in my voice, I told her, "Sure, I'll go." Moments later, I climbed into the backseat of their car, and we headed over to Sharon's home.

Feeling the need to be the brakeman on the train, I announced in the first minute of the drive, "Under no circumstances are we buying a puppy today." I knew full well that visiting a litter of puppies often resulted in bringing one home, and I was dead-set against that. I had my principles, you know. *This may be an emotional decision*, I thought, *but I'm not going to let it be a first-visit emotional decision.* My parents agreed. We were going "just to look."

Sure enough, it took less than fifteen minutes to arrive at the entrance of Sharon's neighborhood. It was a newer development of nice homes set amidst a picturesque landscape of rolling hills and trees at the point where suburban meets rural.

We stopped-and-started our way down the street, scanning each house to locate the right address. Eventually we came to it, about halfway down on the right side. As if on cue, the conversation in the car went mute, from talking to taking in. The home was generously sized and well-maintained, sitting on the side of a hill overlooking a couple acres of lawn, marsh, and trees. A long driveway paved a meandering descent from the street to the house.

My dad slowly turned the car across the threshold of the driveway. In unison, our eyes naturally followed the path ahead to its termination at the mouth of a three-car attached garage.

The single door on the right was open, and some sort of large cushion looked to be lying on the ground just inside the door.

Before another byte of information could be absorbed, up from that seemingly lifeless cushion popped the little head of a Lab puppy, its dark eyes and nose looking like burnt holes in a blanket against the cream-colored background of its face. The pup, appearing a bit groggy from a nap, locked its gaze on our car coming down the driveway.

"Oh my goodness!" I let out incredulously. "It looks just like Ben!"

We travelled the remaining distance down the driveway, all the while never diverting our attention from the eyes staring back at us from what turned out to be a denim-blue, nest-style dog bed.

By this time, the sound of our engine set off a wail of yaps and woofs from farther inside the garage. In short order, the sources of those barks came bounding out the garage door, a mismatched trio of small, medium, and large adult dogs—one a terrier, another an Airedale, and the third a white Labrador, whose coat looked slightly on the scraggly side. I surmised that the latter must be Mom.

During all the commotion, the puppy that had been tracking us down the driveway scaled over the wall of the dog bed to join the welcoming party. As we got out of the car, we could now see that there was one more puppy in the dog bed, this one larger and whiter, and sleepily trying to decide whether our arrival was worth getting up for.

With all manner of dogs excitedly circling about to investigate the visitors, we never made it over to the front door to ring the doorbell. We didn't have to. Just then, Sharon and her family came out, extending hands and smiles to us in the driveway.

Sharon herself appeared to be about my age. Fit and

energetic, she oozed fun and moxie, like the cheerleader with smarts who had graduated to her new roles of mom and vet and loved it. Her two daughters, in their early teens or thereabouts, were equally bright and vivacious and were multitasking between picking up and putting down the puppies and coming in and out of the conversation.

The counterweight to this bubbling bundle of girlhood was Sharon's husband, Doug. A less prolific talker, yet with an equally sharp bearing, Doug was not quite the antithesis of his wife and daughters, but rather appeared to be the stabilizing agent amongst them.

As I stood on the edge of the driveway, listening and engaging in the back-and-forth, my eyes invariably returned to follow the movement of the puppies underfoot. I had subconsciously entered full-examination mode, where every detail and trait of the pups was being observed and interpreted. Out of the corner of my eye, I also kept watch on the puppies' mother, Frostee, a sweetheart of a dog who looked worse for the wear after her first crack at motherhood. Her thinning coat, saggy underside, and generally tired appearance were all part of the demands of being a mom, Sharon told us empathetically.

Regardless of Frostee's condition, her genes had been passed to these puppies, and I tried to ascertain from her build and temperament how they might turn out someday. Frostee had all the signature features of a Ridge View Lab—the pleasant face, the pretty eyes, the sweet disposition, the athletic body. If her offspring grew up to be anything like her, any future owner would be getting quite a Lab.

Sharon's daughters had fitted each puppy in the litter with a different-colored collar in order to tell them apart, but this was no longer necessary with these final two. The male, whom the girls had affectionately named Waldo, was a big boy wrapped in a beautiful all-white coat. There was nothing small or unattractive about Waldo. His paws looked like large paddles ready-made for swimming. His body and head were in perfect proportion; his gorgeous face like something you'd see in a magazine ad. He was your prototypical heart-melter.

The female with the purple collar was named Dori. She was significantly smaller than Waldo, but still in good proportion for her diminutive size. Sharon told us that this little girl was the runt of the litter. You wouldn't have known it by her personality though—she was running here and there, picking on Waldo one minute and playing with the bigger dogs the next. It was obvious that Dori was the doer and Waldo the relaxer.

One of our givens for any new puppy was that we'd get another male. Lab Legend stated, and then was confirmed in our minds by Ben, that males were generally more affectionate than females. The females, while smart and trainable and good hunters, could . . . well, they could be a little snitty.

The problem with Waldo was that while he was beautiful, he seemed a bit lazy and uncoordinated. Maybe even a little light between the ears. After having a dog like Ben, who from birth was nothing if not serious, smart, and focused, it was slightly disconcerting to watch Waldo all splayed out on the grass, putting up little resistance to Dori's persistent henpecking. He stumbled around and quickly lost interest when I crouched down to toss a toy for him to retrieve. My sense was that he was the kind of dog that would be happy to lie around most of the day waiting for his next meal. I could see myself forever viewing him as an underachiever compared to Ben.

Because we were there and everyone was still talking away, I figured I would put the female through a few paces as well.

Dori was very different from Waldo. Her coat was not all white but more of a light cream color with the exception of her ears, which looked like they had been dipped in a jar of honey. As for personality, she was full of it. Super alert, super smart, ready to play, ready for anything. When I threw the toy for her, she ran after it like she meant it. After a few minutes with her, it made perfect sense that she had been the first one up, spying us all the way down the driveway.

This little girl has a lot of life, I thought. *She's Type A and I'm Type B . . . and feeling Type C right now after losing Ben.* Remembering the conventional puppy-picking wisdom to select a dog with an energy level similar to mine, it seemed that either pup was a mismatch for me.

While I couldn't get Waldo motivated, I did notice that Dori's drive settled down. One minute she'd be playing at full speed, the next she would be lying down beside me or holding still in my arms. It was clear that Sharon and her daughters' constant handling of these puppies over the last seven weeks had socialized them well.

My friend Daniel was right—these were some great-looking, well-adjusted puppies with Ridge View written all over them. No doubt about that. After lacking interest in even seeing the puppies, I was glad we had come. If nothing else, I figured we had done our due diligence. We had asked plenty of questions. I had given the pups a good once-over. The bottom line though, as we said good-bye after the two-hour visit, was that we wanted another male, and unfortunately, the one male that was available just seemed a bit too passive for us. Getting a female, especially one that was so lively, was just too big a departure from "the plan."

At least that's what I was thinking when we drove away. What

I didn't know—but probably should have—was that my mother was thinking something completely different.

CHAPTER 19

A LITTLE BIT O' GRACE

That evening my whole family gathered at my brother's house for a birthday dinner. There was some conversation early on about the puppies, but that didn't last long—this birthday, I should have guessed, was destined to be all about Ben.

There were the cards that expressed how fond they were of Ben and how much they missed him and how much they knew I missed him. And then there were the two presents, both of which were picture frames.

The first featured a large photograph of Ben standing on one of his favorite places, the rugged coastline of Lake Superior, with our cabin in the background. Written above the picture was the term of endearment that I often whispered to him—"That's my boy." Underneath the photo was his birth date and that unforgettable date two months ago when we had put him down.

The dozen or more smaller pictures of Ben and me surrounding the main photograph served as snapshots of our life together. There I was in one, kneeled down in a grassy field, shotgun in one hand and pheasant in the other, with Ben sitting beside me after another memorable hunt. There he was in another, in his signature position, fast asleep on the couch with his head resting on my thigh.

I unwrapped the second frame to find a photo of Ben and me taken from behind and with my arm around him, sitting atop a ridge overlooking Lake Superior and the forest below in peak autumn color. It was at once a dramatic and soulful portrait— man and dog contemplating creation from the top of the world. Knowing Ben, he probably was doing just that.

Above the photo was a short poem by Wilbur D. Nesbit stitched into needlepoint fabric. As I read each line, a lump grew larger and larger in my throat.

All to myself I think of you—
Think of the things we used to do,
Think of the things we used to say,
Think of each happy yesterday;
Sometimes I sigh and sometimes I smile,
But I keep each olden, golden while,
All to myself.

I swallowed hard and could feel my eyes welling up in the now-silent room. I kept my head down, trying to resist tears as I recalled the myriad of memories with Ben prompted by these words and pictures. I had received some special gifts in my life—that dog sled for Christmas back when I was a boy comes to mind—but these framed photos were even more special than that. They illustrated and articulated a most cherished relationship over an entire era of my life. It was a bygone era, but a wonderful and unforgettable one indeed.

The evening came to a close, and as I drove home in the dark through the quiet streets around the lake, I reflected on how the gathering had been more memorial service than birthday party.

That was fine by me. We had yet to do something special to remember Ben—a headstone hadn't been placed in the yard; his ashes hadn't been spread or buried. I can't quite say why, but those kinds of memorials didn't feel like something we would do. But this evening did, and for the first time since Ben's death, good memories outweighed the bad.

* * *

The next morning was Sunday, two months to the day since losing Ben. After church concluded, I convened with my parents to see what their plans were for the rest of the day. It didn't take long for them to say that they wanted to go see the puppies again. They had a different look in their eyes today, a settledness, like they were at peace. Something told me that the visit today wasn't going to be about seeing the puppies but rather bringing one home.

A few hours later I found myself again in the backseat of their car on the way to Sharon's. I wasn't interested in going back. But my hand was being forced. I knew my parents were not going to return home empty-handed after a second visit; and therefore, if I wanted any say as to which puppy would be our next family member, I'd better be there whether I felt like it or not.

The conversation during the ride over confirmed my hunch. It became clear that my folks had put plenty of thought and discussion into this, as evidenced by my dad floating the idea of getting the female so as to avoid future comparisons with Ben. This was news to me. Here I was thinking we were on a quest to find another Ben, and now they're telling me we should purposely do something different. Go figure.

After having had a male for so long, the thought of getting a female transported me into an unknown zone. The one time that we had owned a female—Tinka, the Siberian husky—was ages ago, resulting in fuzzy memories of heat cycles and whatever else went along with owning a female dog. My ignorance left me imagining fending off neighborhood male dogs looking for love, and having to stay home from "the best hunting trip ever" because my dog happened to be in heat that weekend.

And while Dori did have that signature Ridge View look, she had a much lighter coat than Ben's and I was definitely partial to Ben's buff color. She also had a small cowlick on one side of her coat. Ben's coat was perfect. And Dori was small. Ben was eighty-five pounds, strapping, athletic and able to leap over tall buildings. This little girl seemed so . . . little.

I brought up every last objection and my parents fended them all off with an irrepressible optimism that I had never seen in them before. Dori's light color was "so minor," her cowlick was my being "too perfectionistic," her Type-A personality was "good because it will be different from Ben."

They were *never* like this. Both of them were old-school, Depression-era realists, much more apt to focus on risk than reward. I was especially surprised at my mother. When it came to making major decisions, she tended to focus on what could go wrong and frequently cautioned against moving too quickly. But suddenly when it came to these puppies, she had become all certain and decisive and upbeat. Usually I was the look-on-the-upside one of the three of us, but there I sat in the backseat feeling as if the roles had reversed. I had my foot on the brake while they were stepping on the gas.

The car neared Sharon's, and as if perfectly timed to coincide with our arrival, my mother concluded the back-and-forth by saying, "David, it's no coincidence that there are two Ridge View puppies available right now this close to home."

If there ever was a debate ender, this was it. The supernatural had just been injected into the conversation. In other words, this whole thing was beyond mere chance, luck, or coincidence. There was something bigger and higher going on here. I felt like Moses hearing the thunder from above on Mount Sinai. Better be quiet, keep your head down, listen, and obey. What was I going to say anyway? I had to admit that the circumstances leading us here seemed way beyond random happenstance.

My dad put the car in park at the bottom of Sharon's driveway and a nearly identical scene repeated itself from the day before. First the onrush of three dogs and two puppies. Then Sharon's family emerging from the house full of smiles. Next, conversation in the front yard with the dogs playing underfoot. Finally, my kneeling down to put the pups through a few paces.

Waldo was the same Waldo. Big boy, good-natured, laid back. I'm sure if he could have talked, he would have said something like, "Chasing after that retrieving dummy that you just threw for me looks like fun . . . but so is lying here in the grass."

And Dori was the same Dori. Alert, driven, sharp as a tack. She fetched the retrieving dummy as if her life depended on it. And when she got tired, she wanted to lie in my lap. I had to admit, this little girl was pretty adorable . . . even with the cowlick and light-colored coat. Ahem.

Sharon invited us inside to show us some pictures of the puppies. "This one was taken on April 11, the day they were born." I looked at the tiny pups, blind and piled on Frostee, who appeared as if she had just returned from the front lines. Poor thing.

After looking at the pictures, I asked Sharon when Frostee had been bred with Higgins, the puppies' father, whom Donna Reece had sold as an adult dog to a breeder-friend of hers in Wisconsin.

I asked the question for no other reason than I had forgotten how long a female dog carries her pups.

Sharon walked over to her calendar in the kitchen and flipped back the pages. "Let's see, Higgins was here for a few days in early February," she said with her index finger running over the calendar dates. "Yes, he was here from February seventh to the ninth, to be exact."

No sooner had her words entered my ears than I felt a tingling sensation run down my arms. I glanced immediately over at my parents, expecting them to recognize the significance of the dates. They didn't.

"Those were the same days that Ben was diagnosed with prostate cancer," I said with a suppressed tone, so as to not over-play it in front of Sharon.

I could see the wheels turning in my parents' heads as they thought about the unusual timing. I couldn't believe it. *You mean to tell me that just when we were hearing the news about Ben's cancer, these puppies were being conceived?* I inaudibly spoke to myself.

Sharon and Doug stood there looking sympathetic, as if sorry that they had stirred up a bad memory for us. That wasn't the case. I was just trying to fathom how, on the precise days that we were receiving a death sentence for Ben, our potential next dog's life was beginning a few miles away.

The "coincidence" wasn't dwelled on for too long before Sharon, perhaps in an attempt to change the subject, picked up some papers from the counter to show us Frostee's and Higgins' pedigrees. The two pages, one for Frostee, the other for Higgins, looked like the tournament brackets that I had seen so many times during my tennis-playing days. Only the lines on these pages didn't hold the names of one player versus another with the winner advancing to the next round, but rather the names of the sires and dams and offspring—the family tree—going five generations back. The "winner" line on the left side of each page contained Frostee's and Higgins' names.

Still stunned over the timing of the conception, I glanced down at Frostee's pedigree. Of all the names on the sheet, my eyes were drawn almost magnetically to the name Snobear, as if someone had run a yellow highlighter through it. I vividly remembered Snobear from our visits to Donna Reece's kennel in Iowa nine years ago. She was the queen bee . . . lived inside . . . Donna's prized breeding female . . . the matriarch of Westminster champions.

Snobear appeared in Frostee's pedigree just two generations back, which meant that Snobear was Frostee's grandmother. I paused for a second to make sure that the connection I was making was correct. It was. Snobear was also the grandmother of someone else—Ben.

Without saying a word, I quickly switched pages to look at Higgins' pedigree. I went back one generation and then two to see the registered name Ridge View's Gust o' Wind followed in parentheses by the call-name Gus.

I recognized that name right away too. Gus was that serious dog Donna's father had brought across the gravel road from the kennel to demonstrate Gus's hunting ability to me. I would never forget that dog.

There was a more significant reason I wouldn't—Gus was Ben's father.

I didn't collapse on the floor. I didn't cry out in astonishment. I didn't say, "To whom do I write the check for a puppy?" But right then and there in Sharon's kitchen, my heart changed. I stopped resisting . . . and surrendered. It was obvious that something bigger and beyond me was going on, and that there was a different and better plan taking place than the one I had in mind.

My plan had been to get a puppy—a male, from Donna, in the future. My plan was about doing what I thought best, at a time I thought right. But what had become abundantly clear was that something other than my plan was going to be *the plan*, that something beyond luck or coincidence was happening right before my eyes. No mere mortal could have orchestrated all this, from when the puppies were conceived to how closely they were related to Ben.

It would have been unusual enough if all this had fallen into place at Donna's kennel half a country away in Ohio. But to have it happen just a few minutes from our home in Minnesota? What other conclusion could possibly be reached than that God was bestowing His grace on us?

That word *grace*. It's a nice-sounding word, but what exactly did it mean? Was it what my father said before we ate a meal at the family table? Was it the extra strength and calmness that I felt in the midst of pressure-packed situations, like in a close tennis match, when all of a sudden I had the strength and resolve to press on beyond what I normally would be able to endure?

Perhaps, but as a Christian, I had always thought of God's grace as pertaining to the really big things in life when God, based on His own initiative and kindness, gifts something of immeasurable value to us that we do not deserve and cannot earn. It's the kind of "Big Grace" that the apostle Paul talked about in his letter to the Ephesian church.

God, being rich in mercy, because of His great love with which He loved us, even when we were dead in our transgressions, made us alive together with Christ (by grace you have been saved), and raised us up with Him, and seated us with Him in the heavenly places in Christ Jesus, so that in the ages to come He might show the surpassing riches of His grace in kindness toward us in Christ Jesus. For by grace you have been saved through faith; and that not of yourselves, it is the gift of God; not as a result of works, so that no one may boast. (Ephesians 2:4–9)

This had been my view of God's Big Grace—when He saves souls and sustains them through the person and the work of the living, breathing embodiment of His grace, Jesus Christ.

I had known about God's saving grace ever since He had gifted me the faith to believe in Christ back in my mid-twenties. But there had been more Big Grace after that. Day after day, month after month, year after year, God kept giving me strength, help, and desire to press on; to understand and follow Him; to over-come temptation; to be and do what I couldn't be and do on my own. God's grace had made me alive and kept me going. It was grace, grace, and more grace.

During all these years, God's grace had always been about the big things, the important things. But there I stood in Sharon's kitchen being forced to reconsider my understanding of the scope of God's grace. I knew God did Big Grace, but did He really do little grace too? Does He actually involve Himself in the more mundane matters of life and bestow a little bit of grace when one of His creatures is hurting and in need? Does He actually have time and attention to give little grace when war and disease and injustice and sin cry out for Big Grace? Does God's grace actually filter down to finding a new puppy?

How ironic that the answer was found in my go-to verse, the one that I had been clinging to for dear life in this storm.

> May the God of all grace, who called us to His eternal glory by Christ Jesus, after you have suffered a while, perfect, establish, strengthen, and settle you. (1 Peter 5:10 NKJV)

I couldn't believe that I hadn't seen it before — "the God of *all* grace." Why had I not noticed that? God was the God of Big Grace *and* He was the God of little grace *and* He was "the God of all grace" in between.

His Big Grace had saved me through Christ and sustained and sanctified me ever since. And now here was a demonstration of His little grace in leading us to these puppies that were so closely related to Ben, so near to home, just at the right time, so that we could experience a little joy, a little encouragement, a little laughter again. We had "suffered a while." But now the bitter would become a little sweeter and the bumpy would become a little smoother. All because He really was "the God of *all* grace."

But as with any gift, God's grace can either be received or rejected. I had spanned the spectrum over the last few days, from rejecting out of hand the idea of getting one of these puppies, to resisting every step of the way. All of that was washed away now. "Circumstances ascribable to divine intervention" is how one person defined the providence of God. I finally saw that God's providence had brought us to this point, and there was nothing left to do but open my hands and receive His little gift of grace.

"We'll take the female," I told Sharon, grinning at my parents, knowing they heartily concurred. Fifteen minutes later with papers signed, thank-yous given, and good-byes made, we were driving out of Sharon's driveway with Dori in my lap in the backseat. I looked down at her, trying to make myself believe that we were actually bringing home a new puppy that I didn't even know existed three days ago, and one that was so closely related to Ben.

She whimpered for a minute or two, understandably thrown off about being in a new place with new people. This little girl was a-Dori-ble all right, but that wasn't going to be her name.

There could be only one. *Gracie*.

CHAPTER 20

CONSIDERING JOB

It was the morning after, and I woke up in the same room in the same house as I had on that other morning exactly two months ago.

This morning after, however, felt a whole lot different.

We left Sharon's that Sunday afternoon and brought our "Little Bit o' Grace" to my parents', where a procession of family and friends filtered up and down the driveway to offer their "oohs" and "aahs" over the precious bundle of Lab puppy. Before we knew it, bedtime had arrived. With all the new people and places this little girl had experienced in one day, we thought it best that she stay her first night at my parents' rather than being moved to yet another new environment at my house.

I decided to stay there as well, knowing that the first night with a new puppy usually entails varying degrees of sleep deprivation. With my folks being in their seventies and me in my thirties, I felt it my duty to take one for the team, so to speak. And so I descended those same stairs to the same bedroom where I had slept two months ago on the night we put Ben down.

That night, I went downstairs with grief. This time, I had Grace.

She slept in the same spot on the floor near the head of the bed where Ben had always slept. Only this night, she would be in a kennel instead of a dog bed, what with her not being housebroken yet. I took her outside once, maybe twice, during the night, and aside from a whimper or two early on, she hardly made a peep. Either she was really tired or really secure . . . or both.

The night may have been uneventful, but the morning after brought unexpected emotions. Two months ago, I woke up in this room and was immediately overcome by the sting of death. The first thing I had done was look over the side of the bed to see if Ben was actually gone. The nightmare was real. The grief was oppressive; my thoughts and emotions dark and painful.

And yet on this morning after when I looked down to see Gracie by the side of the bed, I didn't experience polar opposite feelings of joy and excitement like some feel-good story where all ends happily ever after. Instead, I saw Gracie and still missed Ben.

It was nothing against her. And it certainly wasn't anything against God's amazing grace in bringing her to us. It's just that I wasn't finished healing, and a new Lab puppy, however pretty and pert, and however closely related to Ben, wasn't going to make it all go away just like that. This morning made me realize that Gracie wasn't going to be the final cure after losing Ben but rather part of the ongoing healing process. There was still more road ahead with perspective to gain and grace to receive.

I cradled Gracie in my arms and carried her upstairs as if delivering a newborn baby to expectant parents. You would think that seventy-somethings might be past the point of getting excited over a new puppy, but that wasn't the case with my folks. They were clearly thrilled about Gracie. And more than ready to embrace having her—far more than I.

In another twist of timing, this Monday was the day we had

chosen a while back to drive up north to our cabin to spend a few days preparing the house for some guests who would be staying there over the summer. Normally, any excuse was a good excuse to get up to our beloved family retreat, and one or more of our family generally did so every few months. But this year no one had been there—not me, not anyone else—during the long ordeal with Ben.

Frankly, I had hardly given a thought to going up to the cabin ever since Ben had become sick. My singular focus to care for him had pushed pretty much everything else right out of mind. And now the prospect of going to the cabin for the first time without him wasn't very appealing. In fact, my parents and I had been feeling a sense of dread. Ben was always a central, even essential, part of going to the cabin. What would the long car ride be like without Ben in the backseat fast asleep with his head across one of our laps? How would we respond when we approached the front door and saw the homemade plaque that read "Benjamin P. Bear"? What would the cabin feel like without Ben's presence in every room? I already knew the answers and didn't care to experience them.

It had been eight months since I had last been to the cabin, the longest span between visits that I could ever remember. That was all the way back to October of last year when Ben and I were there enjoying an extended stay during the waning days of fall. It's a good thing I hadn't known then that it would be my last time with Ben at the cabin. How to come home or carry on with that knowledge?

But now, a first trip back without Ben had suddenly become a first-time visit with Gracie. What portended to be bitter at least had some potential for sweet. And that is exactly how it turned out to be.

With all the hubbub of the last few days, we delayed our departure one day and made the five-hour drive on Tuesday. Once underway, the bitter immediately began to joust with the sweet. I'd instinctively glance in the backseat to look at Ben . . . but there was Gracie. The plaque with Ben's name greeted us at the door . . . but there was Gracie under our feet. Inside, memories and mementos of Ben were everywhere: family pictures with him, dog dishes, his bed, his retrieving dummy, even the two grouse mounted on the wall that he had put to flight and retrieved. The house was Ben all over . . . but there was Gracie, lying on his bed, eating out of his dishes, providing a presence of her own.

I took Gracie down in front of the cabin to the ledge rock shoreline. The massive shelf of rock formed an impenetrable line of defense against the driving winds, frigid waters, and pounding waves of Lake Superior. It must have been the genetic imprint of his Lab forbears in Canada who had lived and worked in similar environs that made Ben look so at home on this hard transition between land and water. He loved roaming the rugged ledges as much as he enjoyed paddling out in the forty-degree water.

Gracie was too little for much exploring, but it was obvious this would be her terrain someday too. At one point, she sat down on the ledge rock in a frog-like pose, her back legs splaying forward between her front legs while gazing out over the churning lake. I stood there watching Gracie but remembering Ben. The bitter and the sweet jousted on.

* * *

Wednesday evening brought one last phone call from Dr. Rivers to tell us the autopsy results. It was odd to be talking with him from the cabin, a place that held only happy memories about

Ben. Things like cancer, death, and autopsies had never been a part of the conversation here.

We had been waiting a long time for the final results with one particular question lingering on our minds: had the surgery made Ben worse?

My question was answered before I even asked. Evidently the hundreds of microseeds implanted in Ben's abdomen had reacted so strongly with his prostate tumor that the surrounding tissue had become highly inflamed. Add to that the toxins released from dying cancer cells and it had all been too much for Ben's system. That would explain the nausea, the vomiting, the malaise, the loss of appetite that Ben exhibited soon after the surgery until his final day.

Dr. Rivers said more, but I didn't hear much of it. By the time the call ended, I felt sick to my stomach. Talk about regret. Talk about self-loathing. I chided myself over the possibility that Ben might have lived longer if I had just stayed home and given him medication to manage his symptoms. Perhaps his final weeks would have been more peaceful and comfortable. Maybe he never would have had those awful seizures.

I lay in bed that night hurting and bewildered. Losing Ben was difficult enough. But knowing my decision had made him worse was unbearable.

I closed my eyes and silently anguished, *Why, God?*

It was a heart cry. The very question implies that God knows my plight and that He has control over all the details. I was pleading with Him to tell me why because I thought that would somehow help.

To be sure, God had already shown me much through this trial. I had seen the ugliness of death. But I had also been reminded of the victory over death and hope of heaven that Jesus Christ offers to all based on His own victory over the grave. I didn't know if this hope applied to Ben, but I was still determined to find out.

I had also seen how God arranges even the little circumstances of life in the remarkable way that we had gotten a new puppy — one that we had done nothing to find, one that was so near our home, and one that was so closely related to Ben.

And I was beginning to understand that God's grace was the explanation for all of it. From His Big Grace in sending Christ to His little grace in giving us Gracie. From the comfort and strength I had been receiving, to the loving and supportive family and friends surrounding me. Even having a great dog like Ben was God's grace. It was all grace, and God was the Master of dispensing it in all His various ways and means.

We drove home from the cabin on Friday, and while I didn't have an answer for my *Why, God?* question, I did have grace . . . and a tangible reminder of that grace was snuggled up next to me in the backseat.

* * *

Ready or not, I had a new puppy to raise. But I felt strangely unprepared, even after having Ben for so many years. I kept trying to remember how I had done things with Ben with regard to housebreaking, socializing, and obedience training. Fortunately, Sharon and her girls had done such a good job with the former two that pretty much all I had to do was get a refresher on the training by rereading Richard Wolters' book, *Game Dog*.

I couldn't believe how much I had forgotten about Wolters' one-block-builds-upon-another progression of training. His plan worked so well with Ben that it had been almost autopilot after the first year, which explained why I now needed some reminders.

Gracie may have been closely related to Ben, but she was a totally different animal (pardon the pun). It's what you hear parents of multiple children say, "We raised them all the same way, but wow, they are so different from each other!" Ben was always serious and mature, wise beyond his years, approaching everything with thoughtfulness. Gracie, smart as a whip and on perpetual high alert, was all about fun. God obviously knew I needed her irrepressible cheer after losing Ben.

When I parked my truck midsummer in the driveway of Mike's dog-training facility for Gracie's first session of bird and gun introduction, I sat in the vehicle for a few moments, pondering where I was and why I was there. If you had told me eight months earlier that I would be unloading a new puppy out of my vehicle at Mike's to start all over, I wouldn't have believed you nor could I have even imagined it.

But there I was a few minutes later watching little Gracie enthusiastically chase through the grass after a wing-clipped pigeon with Mike popping off the starter pistol under his arm. With her laser-like focus on the bird and strong desire to re-trieve, it was readily apparent that she had been born with all the instincts to be a hunting dog. How good a hunting dog, or more specifically, how good in comparison to Ben, only time would tell.

I wish I could have better appreciated those first couple sessions with Mike and Gracie, as it's a unique time that never gets repeated — sort of like watching a child take his or her first steps. The problem was I kept getting distracted by the past, thinking about how Ben had done on the same training drills and how quickly the years had gone by since I first took him to Mike.

But I was also struggling with the present and the future. As

I watched Gracie progress from session to session, from smaller to bigger birds, from softer to louder BOOMS, I kept wondering whether I was going to be able to love this little girl as much as I loved Ben.

Mind you, there was no problem with her. She was a beautiful, bright, affectionate, and obedient puppy. God could not have given us a better dog. It was so obvious that she was His "little bit of grace" to us.

The problem was with me. Could I really believe that losing my precious Ben was not random bad luck but rather a trial that God had allowed and one that He would work together for my good and His glory? Isn't that exactly what this well-known verse says?

> We know that God causes all things to work together for good to those who love God, to those who are called according to His purpose. (Romans 8:28)

If I could just accept—no, *embrace*—my trial with Ben as part of God's higher plan, His bigger purpose, then I could embrace Gracie, who was clearly part of God's plan and purpose. Then I could be at peace. Then I would be healed.

I wasn't really expecting to find out the precise reasons why God had allowed me to lose Ben. If you believe what the Bible teaches—that God is in control over everything and everyone in the universe, from the rising and setting of the sun, to the raising and reducing of nations and rulers, to the opening and closing of the womb, to the establishing of the dates for our births and our deaths, all the way down to the movement of every last atom—the logical conclusion would be that He could have stopped that first cancer cell from growing inside Ben should He have so chosen.

But He didn't. And why not? If He wanted me to learn some life lesson, surely He could have accomplished that some other way which didn't entail losing Ben. The truth is that God never promises—and frankly is not obligated—to explain why He does anything beyond the fact that everything He does is right and brings Him glory in the end.

Reading the book of Job after losing Ben helped me understand this. Job was a blameless man blessed by God with a loving family, good health, and enormous wealth. He had it all. And then out of nowhere, he lost it all—all of his ten children and all of his wealth—to catastrophic events. As if that weren't enough, Job then lost his health, being afflicted with boils all over his body.

If I ever had the thought that no one grieved and suffered like I did over Ben, all I had to do was remember Job.

It's ironic that the reader gets to find out the cause of Job's tragedy because Job never does. The scene in the first two chapters of the book pulls back the curtain in heaven to find God asking Satan, "Have you considered My servant Job? For there is no one like him on the earth, a blameless and upright man, fearing God and turning away from evil" (Job 1:8).

Satan snapped right back, "Does Job fear God for nothing? Have You not made a hedge about him and his house and all that he has, on every side? You have blessed the work of his hands, and his possessions have increased in the land. But put forth Your hand now and touch all that he has; he will surely curse You to Your face" (Job 1:9–11).

What was God's response to this accusation from Satan? Would God take the bait and cause Job to suffer trials in order to prove Himself right? Would God protect Job from experiencing pain and loss?

What God chose to do stretched my understanding of the way

God reigns over His creation and how He regulates the trials we experience for His purposes. The hard truth is that God granted Satan permission to afflict Job — with certain limitations — when He replied to Satan, "Behold, all that he has is in your power, only do not put forth your hand on him" (Job 1:12).

What happened next to Job — losing his children, possessions, and health — is something that you would not wish on your worst enemy. Job was never warned about what was coming, and he never found out why he suffered such devastating loss. Job never knew that he was the object of a divine conflict in which God allowed Satan to kill and destroy everything of Job's, except his wife and life, in order to prove that Job's faith in God was genuine, and thus, God would be glorified.

To his great credit, Job never blamed God, even despite the fact that his wife urged him to do so when she said, "'Do you still hold fast your integrity? Curse God and die!' But he said to her, 'You speak as one of the foolish women speaks. Shall we indeed accept good from God and not accept adversity?' In all this Job did not sin with his lips" (Job 2:9–10).

Job understood that not just the blessings of life come from God but so do the adversities. God is over all and in control of all. He either causes or allows everything that happens. Sometimes He *causes* adversity, as when He took the life of King David's newborn son after David committed adultery. Other times, as with Job, God *allows* adversity by pulling back on the restraint He exercises over sin and evil in our fallen world. To be clear though, the Bible says that God is never the instigator of evil nor does He tempt anyone to sin. But He has given us the freedom to make choices, and sadly, too often we choose to sin and do wrong . . . and yet, only to the extent that God allows.

Job may have been "blameless" and "righteous" but he still

had questions, as anyone would, about why God allowed him to experience such pain and loss. For chapter after chapter, Job and the friends who came to console him went back and forth asking the same question I did: why had God allowed such affliction?

After hearing enough of their faulty human reasoning, God eventually entered the conversation and spoke directly to Job.

Now, I would have thought that God would have just explained to Job what had taken place behind the scenes and why He had allowed this trial. But God did no such thing.

Instead, He asked Job a series of questions — which Job was incapable of answering or understanding — in order that Job might "get it" that God is the all-knowing, all-powerful Creator, Sustainer, and Sovereign of the universe. The point being that if God knew what He was doing with the incomprehensible universe, He surely knew and could be trusted to do the right thing in the life of Job.

Here are just a few of God's unanswerable questions to Job:

> "Where were you when I laid the foundation of the earth? Tell Me, if you have understanding, Who set its measurements? . . . On what were its bases sunk? . . .

> "Have you ever in your life commanded the morning, and caused the dawn to know its place? . . .

> "Have you entered the storehouses of the snow, or have you seen the storehouses of the hail, which I have reserved for the time of distress, for the day of war and battle?" (Job 38:4–6, 12, 22–23)

God was just getting started. Question after question followed, none of which Job could answer. Humbled by the wisdom and power and greatness of God and his own ignorance and impotence, Job could only reply to God with this:

> "Behold, I am insignificant; what can I reply to You? I lay my hand on my mouth. "Once I have spoken, and I will not answer; even twice, and I will add nothing more." . . .

> "I know that You can do all things, and that no purpose of Yours can be thwarted. . . . Therefore I have declared that which I did not understand, things too wonderful for me, which I did not know. . . . Therefore I retract, and I repent in dust and ashes." (Job 40:4–5; 42:2–3, 6)

The story of Job deeply impacted me. I could relate to him, not in comparison to what he suffered, but in what he pondered afterward. I had my own moments of wondering, *Why, God?* But reading about Job helped pull back my perspective from being narrowly focused on my own trial to gaining a broader view that God has His purposes and they are not always knowable.

The conclusion for me was that God is so big and so powerful and so in control that I didn't need or deserve a full explanation for what had taken place with Ben. Instead, I could trust God because He knew exactly what He was doing in my little life, and in the end, He would "cause all things to work together for good."

God did just that in the life of Job as He eventually heaped more blessing on him than ever—ten more children, double the possessions, and many more years of life.

So despite suffering great loss, Job ended up with great gain.

And it wasn't just the gain of children, possessions, and long life. It was the even greater spiritual gain of knowing God more intimately, trusting Him more fully, growing stronger in faith, in character, in wisdom . . . of becoming more pleasing to God.

That God has good purposes for our trials is one of the most challenging things to accept or believe. We see no good in disease, death, loss, and grief, and for the most part, that is true—they are the ugly, yet inevitable, consequences of sin corrupting our world. I didn't need to view the bad as good, but I could see that God is more than able to *take* bad and *make* good. That's what He had done in Job's life, and that's what He was doing in my life as well.

One of my Big Questions had been answered. I didn't have to ask "Why?" of God anymore. I probably would never know the specific reasons God permitted that first cancer cell to multiply inside Ben's body. Whatever the reason behind God causing or allowing me to lose Ben, it was now clear that I wasn't experiencing a random accident, but rather God was in perfect control.

I could trust Him and know that He would take my trial and somehow, someway, turn it into a triumph—for me and for Him.

CHAPTER 21

MY GOOD, HIS GLORY

Gracie was five months old when the cooler breezes heralding fall began to shimmer the September leaves. By now she had completed her six-session course of bird and gun introduction at Mike's and passed with flying colors. In fact, she was exhibiting so much drive and determination that Mike sent me home with a remote training collar, saying rather diplomatically, "You're probably going to need one of these."

It was true, I would. This little girl was a force of nature — perpetually enthusiastic, constantly alert, brimming with personality, and irresistibly adorable. Everyone who encountered her addressed her with a variation of the same word. "What a sweetheart!" "Hi, Sweetie!" "She's so sweet!" If Ben was known for his nobility, Gracie would be for her sweetness. She wanted to be with me, around me, or preferably on me.

I am ashamed to admit that it took me this many months to really start appreciating my new little girl. The healing process had been slow, but the good news is that my wound was closed and didn't need much attention aside from trusting in the remedies that the Healer had provided along the way: comfort in His Word, grace for each day, and hope because of Jesus' victory over sin and death.

We took Gracie up north to the cabin in late September for our annual family vacation, and she fit right in as if she had been a part of us forever. She loved the hikes through the forest overlooking Lake Superior and the walks down the ledge rock shoreline. She even did pretty well on her first few hunts, sniffing the trail ahead and putting the occasional grouse to flight.

The "Benjamin P. Bear" plaque was still there to greet us when we returned to the cabin at the end of the each day, but it didn't pain my stomach anymore. Instead it seemed more of a reminder of what a great dog Ben was and how gracious God had been to give me another one so much like him. It had taken a while, but grief had been overcome by grace.

October came and went, and Gracie had now become a part of my seasons of life. Over the summer and into the fall, there had been the daily walks through the neighborhood, the rides in the car and boat, the swims in the lake . . . the constant presence that Ben always provided. Gracie was already doing what great dogs do—sweetening the journey.

For all the years I had Ben, that journey included a road trip west to South Dakota in early November to join some friends for the first pheasant hunt of the fall. I loaded my car with all the same stuff that I typically brought on trips like this—the same clothes, the same gear, the same shotgun, the same dog kennel. Only this year there was one major difference—Gracie jumped up into the kennel instead of Ben.

The five-hour drive through the small towns and agricultural fields of Minnesota and South Dakota afforded me plenty of time to think. It was ten months ago, on the very first days of the year, in the same town where I was now heading, when I first noticed that something was wrong with Ben.

So much had happened since then. Unfathomable grief, unexpected grace — an unimaginable experience. It was hard for me to believe all I had been through, even though I had just gone through it. I may have been driving in the same car with the same stuff to the same town on the same trip that I took every November, but I was a different person.

And I was still pondering one more Big Question. It's the one that every dog owner wonders about and one that I could not get settled, despite searching long and hard for the answer — where is Ben now?

I know what I *wanted* the answer to be, and I know what the majority of dog lovers would say — that dogs go to heaven — but wanting and wishing weren't enough for me. I needed a sound answer based on truth rather than a heartwarming tale about Rainbow Bridges, Doggie Paradise, and the like.

I scoured the Bible, looking for any shred of evidence about animals in the afterlife. Do they die and simply return to dust, forever annihilated from existence? Do they go to heaven to forever live in the presence of God with angels and believers who put their faith in Christ?

One thing I knew for certain was that animals don't go to hell. Scripture clearly and consistently describes that God-forsaken place as the eternal destination of judgment and torment for Satan, his legion of fallen angels, and men and women who reject God's offer of forgiveness and reconciliation through His Son. Jesus could not have been any more clear when He said, "He who believes in the Son has eternal life; but he who does not obey the Son will not see life, but the wrath of God abides on him" (John 3:36).

How could God pour out His eternal wrath on animals for not obeying the Son when they aren't capable of believing in the Son? How could God hold animals accountable for breaking His laws when they don't even know His laws? No one thinks a lion should be punished for killing an antelope or stealing from another lion. And neither does God.

So hell was out of the question for Ben. But what about the other two options—heaven or annihilation?

I kept going back and forth in my mind. I read what respected Christian scholars said about animals and the afterlife and found there was little consensus, even among them.

Just when I thought I would forever be left wondering and wishing, my perspective on heaven was sharpened through a conversation on my radio show with a former pastor who had written a book on the topic.

Instead of heaven being "up there," as I had always imagined, he pointed out that the Bible says God will someday bring heaven "down here." He referenced that passage in the final pages of Scripture, where we are told God will someday destroy the present earth with fire and then create a new heaven and a new earth.

> Then I saw a new heaven and a new earth; for the first heaven and the first earth passed away, and there is no longer any sea. And I saw the holy city, new Jerusalem, coming down out of heaven from God. . . . And I heard a loud voice from the throne, saying, "Behold, the tabernacle of God is among men, and He will dwell among them, and they shall be His people, and God Himself will be among them, and He will wipe away every tear from their eyes; and there will no longer be any death; there will no longer be any mourning, or crying, or pain; the first things have passed away."

And He who sits on the throne said, "Behold, I am making all things new." (Revelation 21:1–5)

This isn't a picture of saints playing harps on clouds, but rather a new and perfect earth void of sin and suffering, a place where God lives among the people He redeemed. This new earth will be the fulfillment of what God designed and intended for His original creation in the Garden of Eden before Adam and Eve disobeyed God, bringing the corrupting influence of sin upon our world.

What does this have to do with animals in heaven? Well, doesn't it seem reasonable, even probable, that since God created animals to be an important and prominent part of His original perfect earth, that animals will also be a part of His future perfect earth? Count me as one who believes that this is likely. Even more, considering that Christ is earlier described as coming out of heaven on a white horse to rule over earth (Revelation 19:11).

Now, does this mean that Ben will be in heaven, or for that matter, all animals that have died in our present fallen world? I don't know the answer to that question, but after reading the story of Job, I know Who can be trusted to make the right decision. God is the One who created all the animals, and He is the One with the power and authority to bring them to heaven if He wills.

This gave me comfort and confidence. I realized that in the same way I didn't know all the details as to why I lost Ben, I didn't have to know all the details about where he was now. I didn't need to worry about Ben—he was one of God's creatures, and Ben was far more secure in His arms than he ever was in mine. God knows and would do what was best for Ben, for me, for Him. If He thought heaven would be more heavenly for me and more glorifying for Himself by bringing Ben there, I have no doubt He could and would do it. My hope and trust would be in Him. He would work all things together for good.

* * *

I arrived around noon at my friend's farm near Huron, South Dakota. This was a place I had been going to ever since Ben was a puppy. A whole lot of memories had been made here over the years in the field and with the family.

One more friend from nearby arrived, and we caught up with each other for a few minutes in the garage before heading out to walk the acres of grass, trees, and marsh behind the farmhouse. Both friends were well aware that I had lost Ben and were kind to express their sympathies and show interest in Gracie. I shared a bit of the story, but a minute or two wasn't going to do more than scratch the surface. It was enough for now.

We hunted the area behind the house for a couple hours and then drove the gravel road north to another piece of land about ten minutes away. Gracie had done fine on her first pheasant outing, considering she was too little to push through the thick cover and too inexperienced to do much more than stumble across the occasional bird. My hunting expectations would have to be tempered. I was going from partnering with a seasoned pro to a beginner, and it would take years to make up the difference, if ever.

I looked out my car window to the west and estimated we had an hour before the sun would meet the horizon. With light winds and wispy clouds, it was shaping up to be a stunning end of the day in farm country. I had been in places where mountains, trees, and lakes provided the natural drama, but there was drama here too, albeit in a more subtle way. It was the glowing cast of the sun across harvested grain fields and the marshes and waterways that ran through them. It was the abundance of wildlife—deer, pheasant, fox, coyote, hawks, and eagles—and the opportunity to see them in open terrain. It was the simplicity and serenity of the landscape and the lifestyle that accompanies it. It was all of the above that kept me coming back, but most especially, it was the great experiences I had with Ben.

My brief contemplation was brought to a pause by something I recognized in the passing scenery. I slowed my vehicle so I could take a more conscious look. It wasn't a person or an animal that caught my eye, but rather a particular section of the landscape. I had seen this place before, although not from my present vantage point. The various elements quickly congealed in my mind, confirming I was where I thought I was. On the north end was a house and barns shielded by a line of trees on two sides. There was a huge marsh that started by the house and ran due south into a shallow valley shouldered on either side by gradual hills.

I could see the entire scene—the house, the barns, the marsh, the hill on the other side, and the setting sun arcing down toward the fields beyond. This was the last place that I had hunted with Ben on January 3 earlier this year. That was the unforgettable day he had hunted like he knew it would be his last. Pheasant after pheasant he found and pointed, first through the trees by the house and then in the marsh. I had never seen him hunt with such purpose and proficiency.

I thought back to our walking out of the marsh at the end of that day and up the hill to where our vehicles were parked. We had finished just before sunset, having bagged our limit of pheasants. I glanced behind us to see Ben coming up the hill carrying the final rooster, which he had just retrieved. It should have been a perfect day—the mild weather, the close camaraderie, the abundant pheasants, the fantastic dog work by Ben, and the beautiful sunset.

But it wasn't perfect. I hadn't liked the way Ben slowly walked up that hill, and I definitely hadn't liked the way he listlessly lay in his kennel as we packed up the car to head home. I remember thinking how something wasn't right with Ben and how concerned I was.

All of this ran through my mind in an instant upon seeing the view out my window. I drove on past the farm thinking about that last day and all that had happened since then. All the grief. And yet, all of God's grace.

Ten months before, I could have told you that the point of life is not simply to get through unscathed but rather to get right with your Creator and become the person He wants you to be. What I had come to understand is that trials are God's favored means toward this end. Years ago, it had been trials (of the self-inflicted variety) that led me to repentance and faith in Christ to become right with God. And now the crucible of losing Ben had provided the fertile soil for the growth God desired in my life.

I was reminded again of my go-to passage: "May the God of all grace, who called us to His eternal glory by Christ Jesus, after you have suffered a while, perfect, establish, strengthen, and settle you. To Him be the glory and the dominion forever and ever. Amen" (1 Peter 5:10–11 NKJV).

I indeed had suffered for a while. The "God of all grace" had been perfecting, establishing, strengthening, and settling me. Growth had come after grief as a result of grace.

But I really hadn't crossed the line on the last sentence in the passage. It's as if it were hanging there waiting for me to face it. Could I honestly say, even after all I had gone through in losing my beloved Ben, "To Him be the glory and dominion forever and ever. Amen"? Could I thank God for allowing this trial and praise Him for what He had done through it?

Could I "exult in [my] tribulations, knowing that tribulation brings about perseverance; and perseverance, proven character; and proven character, hope" (Romans 5:3–4) as the Apostle Paul urged his fellow believers?

Could I "consider it all joy . . . when you encounter various trials, knowing that the testing of your faith produces endurance. And let endurance have its perfect result, so that you may be perfect and complete, lacking in nothing" (James 1:2-4)?

Of course this kind of response to trials flies in the face of our human reasoning. We deem it self-flagellating to "exult in our tribulations." We think it unrealistic to consider our trials "all joy." We question why God would allow such a situation in the first place by asking, "*If* God is good, why is there so much pain and suffering in my life and in the world?"

We think the wrong way and ask the wrong questions because the trauma of our trials takes us to a low point where it's hard to see God's higher purpose.

But God does have His higher purposes. He declares, "As the heavens are higher than the earth, so are My ways higher than your ways and My thoughts than your thoughts" (Isaiah 55:9).

Many times I had read about the apostle Paul living with a perpetual trial, an unspecified "thorn in the flesh" that he repeatedly asked God to remove. Paul wanted out of this trial, as I wanted out of my trial with Ben. But God told Paul, "My grace is sufficient for you, for [My] power is perfected in [your] weakness" (2 Corinthians 12:9).

Paul apparently got the point that God's grace was sufficient by responding, "Most gladly, therefore, I will rather boast about my weaknesses, so that the power of Christ may dwell in me. Therefore I am well content with weaknesses, with insults, with distresses, with persecutions, with difficulties, for Christ's sake; for when I am weak, then I am strong" (2 Corinthians 12:9–10).

I knew this was the final step of faith God wanted me to take—to be content with my distresses and my difficulties; to be thankful for this trial and to praise Him for it.

I thought back to how God had been present and active during the time I was losing Ben and afterward. Through my loss, through my grief, through my weakness, when everything appeared bleak, God's grace truly had been sufficient. In fact, it had been more than sufficient—it had been amazing.

He gave me passages in His Word to comfort and strengthen me. He gave me a loving family and friends to support me. Above all, He gave me the faith to believe in His Son, Jesus Christ, whose perfect life, atoning death, and victorious resurrection offer hope for the future—a future where sin and death won't corrupt everything.

God also gave me hope for the present and the future, that He would take my trial with Ben and turn it into something good. All I had to do was consider the last ten months to see that this is exactly what God had done. He had used my tribulation to push me toward perseverance and proven character. He had used my suffering to "perfect, establish, strengthen, and settle me." He had increased my empathy toward others going through terminal illness and toward those who had lost their own dog. He had even given me little Gracie.

But the greatest good of all was that God had drawn me closer to Him. I knew Him better now. I trusted and loved Him more. I had a much deeper and greater appreciation for why He had sent His Son into our world.

I know for certain now that none of this good would have happened, at least to the degree it did, had I not gone through this trial, this test. Losing Ben in the prime of his life was one of very few scenarios that could have brought me so low and yet drawn me so close to God. God had seen to it that a whole lot of positives had come out of one big negative. Through great loss, God had given me great gain.

It is a hard truth to believe that God causes all things—even the hard things—to work together for good to those who belong to Him. But that is exactly what He did for me.

Driving down that country road, I had come to realize that this story is about more than Ben and me—it is about God placing a beloved dog in my life to lead me to and satisfy my deepest need for His gospel, His grace.

It was then that I could *finally* say, *"To Him be the glory and the dominion forever and ever. Amen."*

AFTERWORD

God causing all things to work together for my good and His glory didn't end on that gravel road in South Dakota.

It was April 2, one day shy of the second anniversary of losing Ben, and there I sat in my parents' living room on the same couch where I said my final good-bye to him.

I was there because I had something to tell my parents. Something important.

"Dad and Mom, I have decided to ask Brodie to marry me. And I was thinking of doing so tomorrow so that the day will have a happy memory to go with a hard one."

I could tell by the looks on my parents' faces that they were trying to figure out what had happened to me and whether I was really sure about this. Who could blame them?

After all, I was almost forty and had been a fairly contented bachelor for many years. Sure, I had wrestled over the past decade with whether I was the marrying type or a career single, but the matches mostly fell to the latter rather than the former.

And marry Brodie? That may have looked like a foregone conclusion in years gone by, what with our friendship going back over thirty years to our single-digit days. But that was a long shot now, especially after two extended periods of dating had ended in disappointment. The last breakup two years ago, after losing Ben, closed the door for good in Brodie's mind. Carrying on with her during my time of grieving had simply proved too much for me.

What my parents didn't know, and what Brodie had found out

only a short time before, was that something inexplicable had been taking place inside me in recent months. It was a paradigm shift and a major one—God had changed my heart on marriage.

There were no signs in the heavens, no audible voices, no handwriting on the wall. But slowly and surely my mind, my will, and my heart joined in unison with a desire for marriage. And once that Rubicon was crossed, it took only a short time to see what had been obvious to everyone else all along—that Brodie and I were made for each other.

The two of us had a few soul-searching conversations prior to my arrival on my parents' couch, with her surmising that a third go at the dating game might be in the works. But I wasn't playing games this time. I had been changed from the inside, and it was time to take a step of faith and enter into a lifelong covenant.

My mother's only request was that I leave Ben's day for him and propose on the day after, which I did . . . with Gracie and Brodie's Lab Billy underfoot.

Years have passed since we were married that summer, all of them confirmation of God working all things together for good. And then another gift of His grace came our way with the birth of a son we named Tommy. With all the licks he receives from Gracie, he is no doubt destined to be an Egalitarian.

My parents, now in their eighties, are thankfully still with us. They live in the same house overlooking the bay, and that couch is still in their living room next to the window. It's Gracie's spot now whenever she goes over for a visit. My folks love her every bit as much as they loved Ben. And so do I.

Speaking of Ben, he still is never far from my thoughts. How could he be? The memories and pictures I have of him and the lessons God taught me through him keep him perpetually front and center. I only wish that Ben and Gracie could have known each other. They would have been the best of friends.

Gracie is all grown up now. And like Ben, she has become an indispensable part of our seasons of life in Minnesota, whether at home around the lake or up north at the cabin. I will admit that I have begun to feel inklings of dread about losing her someday. Yet I know God's grace will be sufficient.

Until then, I aim to enjoy her every day. She came into her own as a hunting dog a few autumns back. You should see the way she jumps and yelps before I tell her to "hunt 'em up!" It's like Ben's unstoppable determination has been infused into her irrepressible personality. She is a force, as my sister likes to call her—ever happy, ever sweet, ever ready to do something, ever devising how to get into my lap.

In fact, that is where she is right now, curled up between my legs on the ottoman. Her bed on the floor is never close enough, and that is fine by me.

I should finish now because pretty soon she's going to wake up and stare me down with those pretty brown eyes letting me know it's time to go for a walk. And she won't take no for an answer.

She is my little bit o' Grace . . . and my boy Ben would be glad.

ACKNOWLEDGMENTS

The old hymn goes, "To God be the glory, great things He hath done!" He gets the glory for anything I am or this book is.

I also want to thank those through whom God has done great things.

Brett and Sheila Waldman and TRISTAN Publishing: This journey with you has been a joy and blessing beyond what I could have ever imagined. Thank you for all you have done and especially for who you are.

Steve Miller: Your gift of editing made a profound impact on the manuscript . . . and me. I am forever grateful. Thank you, too, LeAnne Hardy and Renee Garrick, for your important and precise editing and proofreading.

Dad and Mom: My love for Ben was but a reflection of your unfailing love for me. I am eternally thankful to be your son.

Brodie: How amazing to look back and see that God was preparing our story in the midst of Ben's story. Thank you for your encouragement, insight, and love.

Marnie, Mark, and John: You all have loved and supported me throughout my life as a brother, and practically as a son.

David Anderson: Only a true friend would have done what you did with our Little Bit o' Grace. I'm thankful and grateful for you.

Sharon Farnell: Your encouragement and counsel, especially when the road ahead was uncertain, will always be appreciated.

Dr. Logan and Dr. Harris: Your help and compassion in our difficult time will never be forgotten. Thanks also to the other vets and staff who did so much for Ben and us.

Dick Van Patten, Donna Reece, Dr. David Brewer, Mike Schulenberg, Nicole Notare, and Pastor Troy Dobbs: Thank you for your thoughtful endorsements.

And finally, to you, the reader: You have honored Ben and me by reading our story. May you cherish your own dog even more. And may you know and experience the God of all grace.

Okay, Gracie, okay—I'll throw the dummy for you now!